International Perspectives on Ethical Educational Leadership

Brandy Yee • Dianne Yee

International Perspectives on Ethical Educational Leadership

Lessons from Workplace Cultures That Have Lost (and Found) Their Way

Brandy Yee
Liberal Studies in Education
California Lutheran University
Thousand Oaks, CA, USA

Dianne Yee
Faculty of Education
Western University
London, ON, Canada

ISBN 978-3-031-70838-1   ISBN 978-3-031-70839-8 (eBook)
https://doi.org/10.1007/978-3-031-70839-8

© The Editor(s) (if applicable) and The Author(s), under exclusive license to Springer Nature Switzerland AG 2024

This work is subject to copyright. All rights are solely and exclusively licensed by the Publisher, whether the whole or part of the material is concerned, specifically the rights of translation, reprinting, reuse of illustrations, recitation, broadcasting, reproduction on microfilms or in any other physical way, and transmission or information storage and retrieval, electronic adaptation, computer software, or by similar or dissimilar methodology now known or hereafter developed.
The use of general descriptive names, registered names, trademarks, service marks, etc. in this publication does not imply, even in the absence of a specific statement, that such names are exempt from the relevant protective laws and regulations and therefore free for general use.
The publisher, the authors and the editors are safe to assume that the advice and information in this book are believed to be true and accurate at the date of publication. Neither the publisher nor the authors or the editors give a warranty, expressed or implied, with respect to the material contained herein or for any errors or omissions that may have been made. The publisher remains neutral with regard to jurisdictional claims in published maps and institutional affiliations.

Cover credit: Pattern © Melisa Hasan

This Palgrave Macmillan imprint is published by the registered company Springer Nature Switzerland AG.
The registered company address is: Gewerbestrasse 11, 6330 Cham, Switzerland

If disposing of this product, please recycle the paper.

This book is dedicated to those ethical educational leaders who serve as the moral compasses of schools and school districts in so many places around the globe. Your unwavering commitment to honesty, fairness, and empathy not only shapes the culture of our educational institutions but also molds the character of generations to come. You are the architects that champion the well-being and academic success of every student and the well-being and professional growth of each of your staff members, guiding decisions with an ethical clarity that resonates through the communities you serve.

Your integrity and personal courage in the face of so many challenges in your daily work inspire us. We hope this book serves as a reflection of your positive impact and a celebration of the ethical path you continue to pave for school leaders of tomorrow.

At the very core of all we do is our family. Your unwavering support, patience, and love have allowed us to chase our dreams—paving the way for you far surpasses anything we have ever done. We love you.

With sincere respect,
Brandy and Dianne

Contents

1 **Ethical Leadership in Education Systems**   1
   Introduction: Our "Why"   2
   Purpose and Structure of the Book   3
   Theoretical Foundations and Perspectives   6
   Ethical Educational Leadership Paradigms   9
   Ethical Instructional Leadership   12
   Vignettes of Leadership Practice and the Voices of Impacted Educators   14
   References   15

2 **Healthy and Toxic Workplace and School Cultures**   19
   Workplace Culture   20
   Healthy and Toxic Workplace Cultures   23
   Healthy and Toxic School Cultures   28
   School District Employee Engagement: A Canadian Vignette   37
   References   39

3 **The Influence of Trustees, School Boards, and the Ministry: "Tricky Politics?"**   43
   The Influence of School Boards   45
   Ethical School Board Leadership in the United States   47
   Ethical School Board Leadership in Canada   54
   Ethical School Board Leadership in Finland   61

Ethical School Board Leadership in Germany   69
The Ethical Dilemma of an American School Board Member   77
References   78

4 The Role of Directors and Superintendents: "Lead Learner or CYA/Teflon?"   83
Ethical Leadership Standards for Directors and Superintendents in Canada   84
Ethical Leadership Standards for Directors and Superintendents in the United States   91
Ethical Leadership Standards for Directors and Superintendents in Finland   96
Ethical Leadership Standards for Directors and Superintendents in Germany   101
An American Assistant Superintendent's Ethical Dilemma   108
References   111

5 The Work of School Principals: "Where the Buck Stops!"   115
Ethical Leadership Standards for Principals in Canada   116
Ethical Leadership Standards for Principals in the United States   122
Ethical Leadership Standards for Principals in Germany   124
Ethical Leadership Standards for Principals in Finland   127
"Where the Buck Stops": The Principal's Office   131
References   137

6 Leadership Lessons from Toxic Educational Workplace Cultures   141
Toxic Workplace Cultures   142
Toxic School and School District Cultures   144
One Teacher's Experience   147
One Principal's Experience   151
One Associate Director's Experience   157
References   161

7 Leadership Lessons from Healthy Educational Workplace Cultures   163
Healthy Workplace Cultures   164
Healthy School and School District Cultures   165

One Teacher's Experience	166
One Principal's Experience	170
One Superintendent's Experience	174
Next Steps and Future Considerations	178
References	180

Index   181

About the Authors

Brandy Yee holds her PhD from Universität Heidelberg in Germany, studying middle years learning, teaching, and leadership in Germany, Finland, and Canada. At the K-12 level, she has worked for two school boards in Canada as a teacher, district specialist, assistant principal, and principal. Currently she is Associate Dean, Director, and Assistant Professor of Pedagogy and Educational Leadership at California Lutheran University, working with undergraduate and graduate education students. Yee always considers her role to be that of "chief learner" in any educational institution she has worked in and hopes her students and staff have learned as much from her as she has from them.

Dianne Yee holds her PhD from the University of Calgary in Canada, studying ICT learning, teaching, and leadership in New Zealand, the United States, and Canada. At the K-12 level, she has worked for five school boards in Canada as a teacher, counsellor, assistant principal, principal, director, and superintendent. Currently she works with graduate educational leadership students at Western University as an assistant professor and at Royal Roads University as an associate faculty member. Yee is very thankful to her unique and diverse learners for teaching her the most valuable lessons about learning, teaching, and leadership.

CHAPTER 1

Ethical Leadership in Education Systems

Abstract In this introductory chapter, we explain why we believe that considering ethical leadership as it is framed and practiced in various educational systems in Canada, the United States, Germany, and Finland is important. And, we describe the structure of the book. We also provide an overview of key concepts in ethical leadership as they apply to current educational systems, considering historical perspectives and key authors in educational leadership literature—in particular, instructional leadership.

Keywords International perspectives on ethical leadership • Ethical educational leadership • Transformative leadership • Social information processing • Multiple ethical paradigms • Ethic of the profession • Ethical instructional leadership

> "The supreme quality of leadership is integrity."
> —Dwight D. Eisenhower, former US President

In this introductory chapter, we explain why we believe that considering ethical leadership as it is framed and practiced in various educational systems in Canada, the United States, Germany, and Finland is important. And, we describe the structure of the book. We also provide an overview of key concepts in ethical leadership as they apply to current educational systems, considering historical perspectives and key authors in educational leadership literature—in particular, instructional leadership.

INTRODUCTION: OUR "WHY"

In their book on ethical leadership and decision-making in schools which is often a central resource in graduate courses on educational ethics in the United States and Canada, Shapiro and Stefkovich (2022) preface their case studies with the assumption that in dealing with ethical dilemmas, school and district leaders want to do the right thing. They suggest that "what is right" for one person or group may not be right for others. This highlights the view that there are often multiple perspectives related to ethical behavior in school systems. We would agree regarding the complexity of leadership decision-making and the importance of leader reflection on multiple perspectives. For us, key questions are, "Has the leader 'crossed the line' into unethical behavior?" "Is the ministry mandate, or district policy, or association code of conduct vague or silent on the issue?" or "What is the impact of this unethical leader behavior on the culture of the school or school district?"

In organizational development literature, one of the authors who has influenced our leadership work in education is Patrick Lencioni (2002, 2004, 2020). A very powerful storyteller, Lencioni is the president of The Table Group, a consulting firm specializing in executive team development and organizational health. He has written many books but is probably best known for *The Five Dysfunctions of a Team*, a very popular fable that explores work team dynamics and offers solutions to help teams perform better. (Lencioni often uses the term "leadership fable" in his titles.) We have attended conferences where Lencioni has shared his work, and we have read all of his publications. Years ago, after attending one of his sessions and subsequently purchasing several of Patrick's books (*Death by Meeting: A Leadership Fable...about Solving the Most Painful Problem in Business* and *The Five Dysfunctions of a Team*), a supervisor who saw the books on our desk asked if we "were doing okay"—and hoped that the district meetings that they were responsible for were effective. We explained that Lencioni's approach is to provoke leaders' thought and reflection through story and uses the typical language of organizational conversation—which is not necessarily always "politically correct" discourse. And, then we discussed the value of meetings for busy principals and the effectiveness of our district meetings. One of his most recent books, *The Motive: Why so Many Leaders Abdicate Their Most Important*

Responsibilities, focuses on assisting leaders to "understand the importance of 'why' they are leading in the first place" (Lencioni, 2020, cover endorsement). Knowing the importance of language and power of story, in our vignettes of leadership practice and in sharing the voices of impacted educators from Canada, the United States, Germany, and Finland, we have "borrowed" from Patrick Lencioni's approach and have used the somewhat raw, and often "cheeky" language, from the leaders and teachers we have worked with. We believe it is very important that we share the power of emotion from their experiences involving ethical leadership and workplace culture.

As we will discuss in this book, in many school systems around the world, school- and system-based leaders have professional codes of ethics that they are expected to comply with in order to create equitable learning for all of their students and effective professional development for all of their staff members. In addition to these key ethical frameworks, as school and district leaders (and parents), our North Star, our typical reflection on the drive home from our school or district office, provides additional ethical clarity. "Is this school leader's behavior good enough for your/my daughter? Are the leadership ethics demonstrated in this situation good enough for your/my grandson?"

Purpose and Structure of the Book

"Who is this for?" is always a fair question to ask as you start to explore a piece of text. We believe that this book will provide current leaders in school systems, or educators who aspire to formal leadership roles, the opportunity to think more deeply about the value of ethical leadership, in their particular contexts, and its impact on the well-being of staff members, the success of students, and the community perceptions of the school and district. Throughout our careers as we have had the opportunity to work, research, and consult in school systems in a number of countries, we gained multiple perspectives and became more knowledgeable about cultural nuances and governance systems in our thinking about leadership—leadership ethics, in particular. And, we became better able to ask critical questions about leadership approaches and frameworks in our current contexts. We think this book provides insight and practical reflection on the connections between ethical leadership and healthy or toxic educational workplace cultures, through the voice and reflection of the teachers, principals, and district leaders in Canada, the United States, Germany, and Finland. We have also come to understand that ethical leadership at various levels of the education system contributes to positive outcomes for students and staff members. However, in the literature on transformational leadership—for example, Hallinger (2003) or transformative leadership—for example, Shields (2020), most authors focus on the work of "the" leader, as opposed to the leadership of a team of leaders or levels of leadership within an organization. That is why we think it is important to consider ethical leadership frameworks and practices in three levels of school system leadership responsibility—the trustee/school board, the district leader, and the school-based leader.

The book is not meant to be read in a linear, lockstep manner—although you might choose to read the chapters in sequence. We have attempted to layer the information on leaders and ethics in Canada, the United States, Germany, and Finland in such a way that the Chap. 3 information on the role of school board members and their governance frameworks also provides an overview of the education system in their countries. (It would be helpful to read that chapter before you read Chap. 4, which discusses district leaders in those countries, or Chap. 5, which focuses on principals in the four countries.) If you are most interested in exploring concepts from organizational psychology and workplace culture and how they apply to school systems, Chap. 2 is the place to begin. If you want to delve into the examples of what we consider to be ethical leadership and healthy educational workplace cultures, go to Chap. 7. On the other hand, if you wish to consider leadership which may not be ethical and toxic educational workplace cultures, Chap. 6 provides those examples. Finally, each of the chapters includes a vignette related to leadership ethics and questions designed for personal reflection or for further dialogue with others; so you might also want to specifically look at the vignettes and questions provided.

The book is not meant to replace current key educational leadership texts: such as the work of Shapiro and Stefkovich (2022) whose multiparadigm framework for leadership ethics we reference and whose scenarios have sparked valuable debate in our graduate educational leadership courses; or, Shields' (2020) transformative leadership theory which we believe provides valuable insights into leadership ethics and effective change processes. Because of our formal training in educational psychology and our practical experience which required understanding of psychological concepts to solve complex leadership issues, we introduce readers to the work of organizational psychologists such as Edgar Schein (2017) and Bob Sutton (2017), but there is much more to be investigated regarding the connections between the disciplines of educational leadership and organizational psychology. Throughout our considerable work with diverse student and educator groups, we know the importance of thoughtful discussion and clear action regarding diversity, equity, and inclusion (DEI) in school systems. We believe that over the course of our careers some individual and systemic improvements have been made; but, "we certainly are not there yet." This is not a book focused on DEI; however, we do provide examples of ethical leadership frameworks and practices which support DEI in the four countries we discuss.

Some of the key concepts explored in this book include:

- Ethical leadership in education promotes fair and equitable access to school and district resources for everyone, regardless of their role or background (Branson, & Gross, 2014; Shields, 2020).

- Ethical school leaders are able to integrate moral and ethical principles into their self-concept and into their daily decision-making, improving staff member satisfaction through integrity, fairness, transparency, and empowerment (Conroy & Ehrensal, 2021; Shapiro & Stefkovich, 2022).

- Ethical leaders nurture a positive, ethical climate in their schools through their actions, which can inspire staff members to follow and provide additional support for their leadership (Ahmad et al., 2017; Conroy & Ehrensal, 2021; Duignan, 2007).

- Ethical leadership approaches foster healthy workplace cultures and increase staff members' readiness to embrace change (Metwally et al., 2019).

- Ethical leadership approaches enhance school district performance and credibility by integrating moral values into school and district practices (Deal & Peterson, 2010; Guo, 2022; Tsai, 2011).

- Ethical school leadership approaches/practices and healthy workplace cultures are closely aligned (Arar & Saiti, 2022).

- The school principal typically plays the role of change agent in establishing and sustaining an ethical culture in their school (Cherkowski et al., 2015; Epitropoulos, 2019).

We hope that you will leave this book with a deeper understanding of these concepts related to ethical educational leadership and with further questions that you wish to debate with your colleagues.

Theoretical Foundations and Perspectives

The ethics of leadership in education has been discussed for many years. Foster (1986) expressed the seriousness and importance of ethics in educational leadership when he wrote, "Each administrative decision carries with it a restructuring of human life; that is why administration at its heart is the resolution of moral dilemmas" (p. 33).

Over the past two decades, organizational development researchers have established the connection between ethical leadership and positive employee and organizational outcomes (Tsai, 2011). Research from Ahmad et al. (2017) reported in the *European Scientific Journal* indicates ethical leadership motivates employees and improves their attitudes and behaviors. It does so by modeling appropriate conduct through personal actions and interpersonal relationships promoted via two-way communication, reinforcement, and decision-making.

In terms of the relationship of ethical leadership to the larger body of leadership theory, the following are among the leading theories with a clear focus on ethics (Ahmad et al., 2017):

- Servant Leadership Theory: Leaders attend to the needs of their followers by nurturing, defending, and empowering them. Servant leaders also inspire their followers to act as servant leaders themselves.
- Authentic Leadership Theory: Leaders behave according to strong, positive values and are consistent in their words and actions. They have a follower orientation and social motivation. Characteristics of authentic leaders include openness, self-awareness, confidence, optimism, resilience, and concern for others.
- Spiritual Leadership Theory: Leaders are ethical, respectful, and compassionate, enhancing the spiritual meaning of their followers' work. Spiritual leaders communicate a vision to their followers to serve a higher or moral purpose, whether or not that purpose has a religious connotation.
- Transformational Leadership Theory: Leaders focus on supporting and motivating followers intellectually, with a focus on the common

good over individual interests. Leaders communicate an inspiring and idealized vision of the organization's goals.

Of note, historically, leadership theory has differentiated transformational leadership into two sub-types. The authentic transformational leader is genuine, ethical, and uses power and authority for the good of others and the community as a whole. Conversely, pseudo-transformational leaders use authority for self-interest, lack morality, and are power-oriented (Bass & Steidlmeier, 1999)—and are not ethical in their leadership approaches.

From an educational leadership perspective, we would also suggest that the transformative leadership work of Carolyn Shields (2020) provides a very helpful framework for enacting ethical leadership with its focus on leaders creating equitable, inclusive, democratic, and socially just schools. Transformative leadership is often confused with transformational leadership because both theories have beginnings in the work of James McGregor Burns and his concept of transforming leadership. The leadership tenet Shields describes as a "call to exhibit moral courage" (p. 4) is particularly aligned with our perspectives regarding ethical leadership. Ethical educational leaders consistently model the values of honesty, fairness, responsibility, respect, and compassion. In any given difficult situation, they are able to identify the ethical considerations involved in their leadership decisions and actions—and to determine, if there are conflicting values, which needs to take priority.

Ethical leadership certainly informs the approaches taken by education leaders and their daily work in schools and districts; and some researchers have begun to articulate the nature and impact of unethical leadership behavior (Treviño et al., 2014). The theory of employee moral disengagement, which was first introduced by Albert Bandura in the 1980s (as an extension of his social cognitive theory), describes set of eight interrelated cognitive mechanisms that facilitate unethical behavior in organizations (Moore et al., 2012). Typical school districts provide a variety of opportunities for moral disengagement which are relevant to our discussion:

> [districts] tend to be hierarchical, providing opportunities for the displacement of responsibility; work is often undertaken within teams, providing opportunities for the diffusion of responsibility; organizational membership automatically defines the boundaries of an in-group, providing opportunities for moral justification (to protect the organization) and the cognitive

minimization of the consequences of one's actions for those who are outside the organization (out-group). (p. 11)

Zhang et al. (2018) have expanded the notion of ethical leadership based on the concept of social information processing (SIP):

> Individuals' social environment helps construct meaning directly through the guidance of socially acceptable beliefs, needs, attitudes, and reasons impinging on actions…Second, social influence and context focus individuals' attention on certain specific information, which makes the information more salient, raises expectations, and highlights the logical consequences of individual behaviors. (p. 2)

They describe several potential impacts of ethical leader behavior on followers' ethical actions and decision-making. When ethical leaders demonstrate honesty, fairness, and consideration in their actions and decision-making, it generates positive emotions in followers. Thus, by leaders' modeling ethical behavior and providing positive examples, followers are more likely to demonstrate moral emotions and to be fair and helpful to others. Making clear connections to school culture, according to SIP theory, one of the important sources of information is an individual's immediate social environment, which influences their attitudes and behaviors. Through their actions and decision-making, school- and district-based leaders are able to impact and to nurture an ethical and moral climate and culture in their schools and districts. At the organizational level, Treviño et al. (2014) explain that formal systems, including decision-making processes, organizational structure, and performance management systems are important components. "Because people in organizations pay such close attention to what is rewarded and what is disciplined, the performance management system—including setting goals and tying rewards to those goals—is particularly important" (p. 641).

According to Brown and Treviño (2006), ethical leadership needs to include the characteristics of both the "moral person" and "moral manager." The "moral person" component of ethical leadership considers the traits and/or character of the leader such as honesty, integrity, truthfulness, openness to input, concern for others, and being respectful and principled in decision-making (Treviño et al., 2014). The "moral manager" component of ethical leadership behavior deals with how leaders use their managerial power and leadership position to encourage and promote ethical standards and ethical behaviors in their workplace. Ethical leaders must embody the traits of both the strong moral manager and the moral person (Brown & Mitchell, 2010). Ethics, as such, is an important part of the leader self-concept as well as the guiding principle for every decision and action of school leaders; this is a very important consideration in understanding our perspectives related to ethical school leader behavior and healthy versus toxic school cultures. Although it is obvious that school leaders are both implicitly and explicitly charged with being ethical, the moral culture of the school is often set through the relationships between principals and members of their school community (Shapiro & Stefkovich, 2022).

Ethical Educational Leadership Paradigms

Over the past 20 years, educational researchers have articulated several different paradigms/perspectives for understanding and interpreting ethical leadership in schools. "Taken together, the ethics of justice, critique, care, community, and profession can serve as an interconnected model or framework for ethical school leadership" (Cherkowski et al., 2015, p. 4). The ethics framework of Shapiro and Stefkovich (2022), which we reference throughout this book, originated in the work of American researcher, Robert Starratt (1991), who identified the ethics of justice, care, and critique as part of a framework to assist educational leaders to understand and cope with the multidimensional nature of their daily work. At that time, he envisioned the "proactive position of an ethics of educational administration…namely the building of an ethical school as an integral part of a national effort to restructure schools" (p. 199). Subsequently Canadian researchers, Langlois and LaPointe (2007) have validated Starratt's work empirically in different cultural and linguistic settings—for example, their studies of leadership in linguistic minority school settings and the ethic of critique in the context of the struggle to protect the linguistic and cultural identity of French-speaking educators. They have written extensively about ethics and leadership; and Langlois, working with colleagues at the Université Laval, has developed *The Ethical Leadership Questionnaire (EQL)*, a tool to measure ethical leadership as demonstrated in the ethical dilemmas encountered as part of daily leadership practice. This instrument is framed by the ethic of justice, of care, and of critique (Langlois et al., 2014).

Shapiro and Stefkovich (2022) describe the complexity of ethical leadership through four leadership paradigms (i.e., the ethic of justice, the ethic of care, the ethic of critique, and the ethic of the profession) as dilemmas in today's challenging and diverse society. Similar to Shapiro and Stefkovich, we agree "that we all [must] become reflective practitioners when attempting to solve ethical dilemmas" (p. xv).

Considering Shapiro and Stefkovich's (2022) framework, the ethic of justice takes into account a wide variety of issues. Viewing ethical dilemmas from this paradigm or perspective, leaders might consider questions related to fairness, equity and justice as well as the rule of law. "These may include, but are certainly not limited to, questions related to issues of equity and equality; the fairness of rules, laws, and policies; whether laws are absolute, and if exceptions are to be made, under what circumstances; and the rights of individuals versus the greater good of the community" (p. 13).

The ethic of critique, aligned with critical theory, focuses leaders on the inequities in schools, as well as in society in general. This ethic requires leaders to engage with the hard questions regarding social class, race, gender, and other areas of difference:

> Who makes the laws? Who benefits from the law, rule, or policy? Who has the power? Who are the silenced voices? This approach to ethical dilemmas then asks educators to go beyond questioning and critical analysis to examine and grapple with those possibilities that could enable all children, whatever their social class, race, or gender, to have opportunities to grow, learn, and achieve. (Shapiro & Stefkovich, 2022, p. 16)

The ethic of care, which has been very prominent in our school-based leadership experience, provides a lens for responding to complex moral problems facing educational leaders in their daily work. Shapiro and Stefkovich (2022) explain that the ethic of care is complex and intricate in that it generally deals with emotions. Viewing ethical dilemmas through the ethic of care may prompt questions related to how educators assist students in meeting their needs and developing solutions to problems will reflect a concern for others as part of decision-making.

> This ethic asks that individuals consider the consequences of their decisions and actions. It asks them to consider questions such as: Who will benefit from what I decide? Who will be hurt by my actions? What are the long-

term effects of a decision I make today? And if I am helped by someone now, what should I do in the future about giving back to this individual or to society in general?. (pp. 19–20)

The ethic of care also requires educational leaders to consider key values such as relational trust and loyalty.

In their many years of researching ethical educational leadership, Shapiro and Stefkovich (2022) uncovered a gap in the literature which led them to articulate the ethic of the profession. Their perspective was that "All too frequently, the ethic of the profession is seen as simply a part of the justice paradigm" (p. 11). In their framework, professional ethics involves "those moral aspects unique to the profession and the questions that arise as educational leaders become more aware of their own personal and professional codes of ethics" (p. 20). They suggest that the ethical codes prescribed by the provinces/states and professional associations are generally limited in that they are often idealistic and "somewhat removed from the day-to-day personal and professional dilemmas which educational leaders face" (p. 23). (In later chapters of our book, we provide specific examples of ethical codes that have been developed in Canada, the United States, Germany, and Finland for the leaders who have a significant impact on schools—school board trustees, directors and superintendents, and school principals.) In responding to the ethic of the profession, leaders must further develop their reflective nature and their understanding of themselves, as well as others. "These understandings necessitate that administrators reflect on concepts such as what they perceive to be right or wrong and good or bad, who they are as professionals and as human beings, how they make decisions, and why they make the decisions they do" (p. 25). Based on our experience with educational leaders and school systems in a variety of international contexts, our perspective is that the history and culture of education systems have significant impact on how leaders adhere to these personal ethical codes.

Finally, from Furman's (2004) perspective, (which Shapiro and Stefkovich reference in their books) an ethic of community considers principles of collaborative relationships and communal processes, emphasizing the communal over the individual.

The clearly articulated framework from Shapiro and Stefkovich (2022) calls on ethical educational leaders to place students at the center of the ethical decision-making process (p. 28).

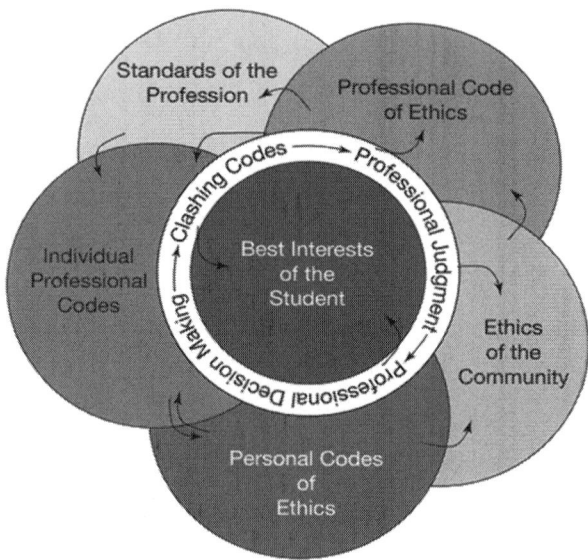

Fig. 1.1 The ethic of the profession. (Note: From *Ethical Leadership and Decision Making in Education: Applying Theoretical Perspectives to Complex Dilemmas (5th ed.)* (p. 28), by J. Shapiro and J. Stefkovich, 2022, Taylor & Francis. Copyright 2022 by Taylor & Francis. Reprinted with permission)

As illustrated in their diagrammatic representation of the ethic of the profession (see Fig. 1.1), "In educational leadership, we believe that if there is a moral imperative for the profession, it is to serve the 'best interests of the student'" (Shapiro & Stefkovich, 2022, pp. 26–27)—we agree.

Ethical Instructional Leadership

In Chap. 5, we will examine the work of the school principal considering the influence of the societal context in which their schools and school systems are located. Using the United States, Canada, Germany, and Finland as examples, similarities across countries, as well as differences based on local or national contexts in fostering the ethical leadership of school principals will be discussed. Consideration will be given to the licensure standards for school principals that require an understanding of ethical issues and the expectation for ethical leadership behavior. Many of the principal leadership standards articulate a variety of leadership competencies from visionary leadership, to instructional leadership, to managing financial and human resources, to developing the leadership capacity of staff members... We understand that each of these leadership competencies is considered important in the particular national contexts; but, carefully investigating ethical behavior related to all of these leadership competencies is certainly beyond the scope of our work in this book. With that in mind, we will focus on ethical instructional leadership.

For many years, research-informed literature has linked principals' instructional leadership to positive school outcomes for students and staff members (e.g., Hallinger, 2003 or Robinson & Timperley, 2007). This is an equity-driven approach that promotes excellence for all students, ensuring that each and every student achieves at high levels (Shaked, 2020). Instructional leadership involves leading, coaching, and mentoring to improve teaching and learning. We believe the key is creating a culture where leaders support and challenge teachers to truly maximize learning opportunities for all of their learning community—both children and adults (Timperley, 2011). Ethical instructional leaders keep the whole learning community focused on the learner and the learning.

The key values and beliefs that influence ethical instructional leadership can vary depending on the context of the school or district, as well as the leader's personal beliefs. However, some common values, beliefs, and practices that are often associated with ethical instructional leadership include:

- A commitment to student well-being and academic success as the fundamental value guiding all leadership decisions (Shapiro & Stefkovich, 2022; Shields, 2020)
- Demonstrating an ethic of care as a foundation of leadership practice (Conroy & Ehrensal, 2021; Shapiro & Stefkovich, 2022; Shields, 2020)
- Modelling honesty, transparency, fairness, respect, integrity, and trustworthiness in daily interactions (ten Have, 2023)
- Demonstrating compassion, inclusiveness, and empathy when implementing instructional policies, including considering current political, social, and economic environments (Fullan, 2003; Shields, 2020; Starratt, 2012)
- Modeling ethical instructional beliefs and practices, which followers can translate into their own actions (Shields, 2020; Zhang et al., 2018)

- Demonstrating a sense of personal courage, including a willingness to voice opposition to policies detrimental to students' best interests (Bradley University, 2024; Shields, 2020)
- Expecting ethical behavior from the whole school community (including teachers, school leaders, students, and parents), communicating these standards clearly, and enforcing them uniformly (Bradley University, 2024)
- Integrating ethical values in building trust among other school leaders (Arar & Saiti, 2022)

Overall, ethical instructional leadership involves a commitment to ethical values and beliefs such as compassion, honesty, integrity, and trustworthiness which prioritize student well-being and academic success.

If our decisions as leaders in a school system are focused on the learner and the learning, then what are the professional ethics/moral imperatives that must guide our decision-making, our interactions with our learning community, and our resource allocation?

VIGNETTES OF LEADERSHIP PRACTICE AND THE VOICES OF IMPACTED EDUCATORS

The vignettes of leadership practice in our book are based on experiences of educators in schools and school districts in Canada, the United States, Germany, and Finland. We have made a concerted effort to ensure anonymity and confidentiality of the educators who have shared their experiences and the impacts of leadership ethics on them professionally and personally.

These leadership ethics vignettes, stories, and reflections focus on educators holding a variety of positions in K-12 schools and school districts which are culturally rich with many ethnicities, faiths, and gender perspectives represented. Because of this diversity, we have used "they" as well as the "he/she" gender specific pronouns. And, we have used given names which are representative of the diversity of these school communities. In the vignettes, the text in italics represents the particular language of the educator.

> *"To lead people, walk beside them. As for the best leaders, the people do not notice their existence...When the best leader's work is done, the people say, 'We did it ourselves!'"*
> —Lao Tsu, ancient Chinese philosopher and author

References

Ahmad, I., Gao, Y., & Hali, S. M. (2017). A review of ethical leadership and other ethics- related leadership theories. *European Scientific Journal, ESJ, 13*(29), 10–23. https://doi.org/10.19044/esj.2017.v13n29p10

Arar, K., & Saiti, A. (2022). Ethical leadership, ethical dilemmas and decision making among school administrators. *Equity in Education & Society, 1*(1), 126–141. https://doi.org/10.1177/27526461211070828

Bass, B., & Steidlmeier, P. (1999). Ethics, character, and authentic transformational leadership behavior. *The Leadership Quarterly, 10*(2), 181–217. https://doi.org/10.1016/S1048-9843(99)00016-8

Bradley University. (2024). *Ethical leadership in education*. https://onlinedegrees.bradley.edu/blog/ethical-leadership-in-education/

Branson, C., & Gross, S. (Eds.). (2014). *Handbook of ethical educational leadership* (1st ed.). https://doi.org/10.4324/9780203747582

Brown, M., & Mitchell, M. (2010). Ethical and unethical Leadership: Exploring new avenues for future research. *Business Ethics Quarterly, 20*(4), 583–616. https://doi.org/10.5840/beq201020439

Brown, M., & Treviño, L. (2006). Ethical leadership: A review and future directions. *The Leadership Quarterly, 17*(6), 595–616. https://doi.org/10.1016/j.leaqua.2006.10.004

Cherkowski, S., Walker, K., & Kutsyuruba, B. (2015). Principals' moral agency and ethical decision-Making: Toward a transformational ethics. *International Journal of Education Policy & Leadership, 10*(5), 1–17. http://journals.sfu.ca/ijepl/index.php/ijepl/article/view/149

Conroy, T., & Ehrensal, A. (2021). Values and the ethics of care: Four portraits. *Values and Ethics in Educational Administration, 16*(1), 1–10. https://files.eric.ed.gov/fulltext/EJ1304345.pdf

Deal, T., & Peterson, K. (2010). *Shaping school culture: The heart of leadership*. Jossey-Bass.

Duignan, P. (2007). *Educational leadership: Key challenges and ethical tensions*. Cambridge University Press. https://doi.org/10.1017/CBO9781139168564

Epitropoulos, A. (2019). 10 signs of a toxic school culture. *Educational Leadership, 61*(9). https://www.ascd.org/el/articles/10-signs-of-a-toxic-school-culture

Foster, W. (1986). *Paradigms and promises: New approaches to educational administration*. Prometheus Books.

Fullan, M. (2003). *The moral imperative of school leadership*. Corwin Press.

Furman, G. (2004). The ethic of community. *Journal of Educational Administration, 42*(2), 215–235. https://doi.org/10.1108/09578230410525612

Guo, K. (2022). The relationship between ethical leadership and employee job satisfaction: The mediating role of media richness and perceived organizational transparency. *Frontiers in Psychology, 13*, 1–13. https://www.frontiersin.org/articles/10.3389/fpsyg.2022.885515

Hallinger, P. (2003). Leading educational change: Reflections on the practice of instructional and transformational leadership. *Cambridge Journal of Education, 33*(3), 329–352. https://doi.org/10.1080/0305764032000122005

Langlois, L., & Lapointe, C. (2007). Ethical leadership in Canadian school organizations: Tensions and possibilities. *Educational Management, Administration & Leadership, 35*(2), 247–260. https://doi.org/10.1177/1741143207075391

Langlois, L., Lapointe, C., Valois, P., & Leeuw, A. (2014). Development and validity of the Ethical Leadership Questionnaire. *Journal of Educational Administration, 52*(3), 310–331.

Lencioni, P. (2002). *The five dysfunctions of a team.* Jossey-Bass.

Lencioni, P. (2004). *Death by meeting: A leadership fable...about solving the most painful problem in business.* Jossey-Bass.

Lencioni, P. (2020). *The motive: Why so many leaders abdicate their most important responsibilities.* Jossey-Bass.

Metwally, D., Ruiz-Palomino, P., Metwally, M., & Gartzia, L. (2019). How ethical leadership shapes employees' readiness to change: The mediating role of an organizational culture of effectiveness. *Frontiers in Psychology, 10*, 1–18. https://doi.org/10.3389/fpsyg.2019.02493

Moore, C., Detert, J. R., Klebe Treviño, L., Baker, V. L., & Mayer, D. M. (2012). Why employees do bad things: Moral disengagement and unethical organizational behavior. *Personnel Psychology, 65*(1), 1–48. https://doi.org/10.1111/j.1744-6570.2011.01237.x

Robinson, V., & Timperley, H. (2007). The leadership of the improvement of teaching and learning: Lessons from initiatives with positive outcomes for students. *Australian Journal of Education, 51*(3), 247–262. https://doi.org/10.1177/000494410705100303

Schein, E. (2017). *Organizational culture and leadership* (5th ed.). Wiley.

Shaked, H. (2020). Social justice leadership, instructional leadership, and the goals of schooling. *International Journal of Educational Management, 34*(1), 81–95. https://doi.org/10.1108/IJEM-01-2019-0018

Shapiro, J., & Stefkovich, J. (2022). *Ethical leadership and decision making in education: Applying theoretical perspectives to complex dilemmas* (5th ed.). https://doi.org/10.4324/9781003022862

Shields, C. M. (2020). *Becoming a transformative leader: A guide to creating equitable schools* (1st ed.). https://doi.org/10.4324/9780429261091

Starratt, R. (2012). *Cultivating an ethical school.* Routledge.

Starratt, R. J. (1991). Building an ethical school: A theory for practice in educational leadership. *Educational Administration Quarterly, 27*(2), 185–202. https://doi.org/10.1177/0013161X91027002005

Sutton, R. (2017). *The asshole survival guide: How to deal with people who treat you like dirt.* Houghton Mifflin Harcourt.

ten Have, H. (2023). Ethics education and leadership. *International Journal of Ethics Education, 8,* 1–3. https://doi.org/10.1007/s40889-023-00167-9

Timperley, H. (2011). *Realizing the power of professional learning.* Open University Press.

Treviño, L., Nieuwenboer, N., & Kish-Gephart, J. (2014). (Un)ethical behavior in organizations. *Annual Review of Psychology, 65*(1), 635–660. https://doi.org/10.1146/annurev-psych-113011-143745

Tsai, Y. (2011). Relationship between organizational culture, leadership behavior and job satisfaction. *BMC Health Services Research, 11*(98), 1–9. https://doi.org/10.1186/1472-6963-11-98

Zhang, Y., Zhou, F., & Mao, J. (2018). Ethical leadership and follower moral actions: Investigating an emotional linkage. *Frontiers in Psychology, 9,* 1–11. https://doi.org/10.3389/fpsyg.2018.01881

CHAPTER 2

Healthy and Toxic Workplace and School Cultures

Abstract In this chapter, first we provide an overview of healthy and toxic workplace cultures from an organizational psychology research perspective. Then we consider healthy and toxic school cultures. We explore possible impacts of toxic school and school district cultures on staff member wellness, on employee development and productivity, and on student learning outcomes—as well as parent and community perceptions of school system effectiveness. We also provide a leadership vignette of Canadian school district employee engagement and workplace culture, including questions for reader reflection.

Keywords Organizational psychology • Healthy workplace cultures • Toxic workplace cultures • Healthy school cultures • Toxic school cultures • Employee engagement

> "Pleasure in the job puts perfection in the work."
> —Aristotle, ancient Greek philosopher and polymath

In this chapter, first we provide an overview of healthy and toxic workplace cultures from an organizational psychology research perspective. Then we consider healthy and toxic school cultures. We explore the possible impacts of toxic school and school district cultures on staff-member wellness, on employee development and productivity, and on student learning outcomes—as well as parent and community perceptions of school system effectiveness. We also provide a leadership vignette of Canadian school district employee engagement and workplace culture, including questions for reader reflection.

In Chaps. 6 and 7, we will delve deeply into examples of leadership in both healthy and toxic school and school district cultures to examine how those teaching and learning environments were impacted. These perspectives are based primarily on our experiences in Canadian and American schools and school districts—and in our review of current research. Also, the United States and Canada are where most of the literature regarding school workplace culture has originated, with some research also being conducted in the United Kingdom. At the time of writing, there is very little in the literature regarding healthy or toxic workplace or school cultures in Germany and Finland. As we will explain in subsequent chapters of this book, it is important to note that Finland's education system is generally designed around well-being, with a key focus on the mental health of students and educators; Finnish teachers are known for being highly respected and autonomous in their work, which certainly contributes to their perspectives on well-being. And, the Finnish education system also emphasizes equity, aiming to ensure that all students, regardless of their societal background, can be successful in their school.

It is our hope to provide connections between the ethical educational leadership literature and the organizational psychology literature related to workplace culture. In Chap. 6, we will provide leadership vignettes of toxic school cultures and educator perceptions of the negative impacts on their school communities; and, in Chap. 7, we will focus on leadership vignettes of healthy and collaborative school cultures and educator perceptions of the positive impacts on their school communities.

Workplace Culture

Workplace culture is a concept which includes the beliefs, thought processes, attitudes of the employees, as well as the ideologies and principles of an organization. It is workplace culture which influences how an organization functions and the way employees interact with each other. Workplace culture refers to the general attitude or mindset of the employees which further impacts the ethos of the organization (SHRM, 2023). A number of researchers have done extensive work on organizational culture. In particular, the original work of Edgar Schein (1985), and the continuing work of Schein and his son, Peter, resonates with our perspective on the nature of organizational culture and importance of ethical leadership to build positive workplace cultures.

Edgar Schein, who died in 2023, was a Swiss-born American business theorist and psychologist who was a professor emeritus at the MIT Sloan School of Management. He is world-renowned for his significant contributions to the field of organizational development, particularly in areas of career development, group process consultation, and organizational culture. He was also the bestselling author of *Helping, Humble Inquiry, Humble Consulting*, and *Humble Leadership*. His book, *Organizational Culture and Leadership* (Schein, 1985), is considered a seminal work in the field, outlining his three-tiered model of organizational culture and exploring the intertwined nature of leadership and culture. The fifth edition of this book was published in 2017.

Schein's (1985) model, which often uses an iceberg graphic to illustrate its three layers, clearly articulates the importance of the deep, underlying cultural norms that influence workplace cultures. There are the visible or shallow layers that have some impact on an organization's culture—or which may be some indication of what the culture is actually like. There are also deeper layers which provide a much greater insight into what the culture is actually like (Schein, 2017). *Artifacts*, the top tier, include the constructed environment of an organization, such as its architecture, technology, office layout, dress code, behavior patterns, and public documents such as employee orientation handbooks. *Espoused values*, the middle tier, are the stated norms and values of the organization; they are the reasons and/or rationalizations for why members of the organization behave the way they do. Espoused values would include documents such as company or employee charters, team contracts, and vision and mission statements. Key *underlying assumptions*, the bottom tier, are the typically unconscious patterns and taken-for-granted beliefs, perceptions, thoughts, and feelings that are the source of values and actions in an organization. Underlying beliefs held by employees include assumptions about how they should work with each other. They also include beliefs about what behaviors will actually lead to success or failure in that workplace. Employees' underlying beliefs are the strongest indicator of what a workplace culture is actually like; and this makes them the strongest levers of organizational change. They are also, however, the hardest levers to influence. Schein (2017) argued that leaders are the main architects of organizational culture and that once cultures are formed, they also influence the kind of leadership which is possible. If elements of the culture became toxic or dysfunctional,

Schein believed it was the leader's responsibility to reshape and develop the culture so the organization would be able to grow and adapt to its environment (Schein, 2017).

Workplace culture sets the context for everything an organization does. This culture consists of shared beliefs and values established by leaders and then communicated and reinforced through various methods—ultimately shaping employee perceptions, behaviors, and understanding. As Schein (2017) explained, a strong and healthy workplace culture is a common denominator among the most successful organizations. Ethical leaders in successful organizations "live their cultures" in their daily work and go out of their way to communicate the cultural norms and identities of the organization to employees. They are clear about their own ethical values as well as how the organizational values determine how their organization operates. In contrast, conflicting messages from leaders regarding organizational culture may create distrust and cynicism, which can prompt employees to justify inappropriate actions and behavior; "Cultural inconsistencies may also cause workers to grow discouraged, to believe management is disingenuous, to doubt statements from higher-ups, and to be less inclined to give their best effort" (SHRM, 2023, para. 45).

The Society for Human Resources Management (SHRM) is an American professional human resources membership association headquartered in Alexandria, Virginia. SHRM promotes the role of human resources as a profession and provides education, certification, and networking to its members. SHRM (2023) emphasizes the function of the human resources departments in developing healthy workplace cultures explaining that human resources departments act as "caretakers" of organizational culture:

In carrying out this essential role, all members of the HR team should help build and manage a strong culture by:

- Being a role model for the organization's beliefs.
- Reinforcing organizational values.
- Ensuring that organizational ethics are defined, understood, and practiced.
- Enabling two-way communications and feedback channels.
- Defining roles, responsibilities, and accountabilities.
- Providing continuous learning and training.
- Sustaining reward and recognition systems.
- Encouraging empowerment and teams.

- Recognizing and solving individual and organizational problems and issues. (para. 8).

From our experience as employees in six different school districts, our perspective would be that, in addition to initial employee-hiring strategies, both the onboarding processes and the evaluation philosophy, policy, and practices which typically reside with Human Resource departments significantly impact workplace culture, in both positive and negative ways.

Healthy and Toxic Workplace Cultures

There are a number of American organizational psychology researchers who have done extensive work on healthy and toxic workplace cultures. And, there are many corporate consultants in Canada and the United States who write about and develop training programs related to healthy workplace culture—particularly with current organizational expectations and commitments to diversity, equity, and inclusion (DEI) initiatives. Many universities in those countries are developing graduate level programs focusing on DEI leadership, and most organizations have developed new positions or departments with a focus on implementing DEI policy. As is typical, and considering Schein's (2017) work, there are still considerable gaps between espoused values and enacted policy related to DEI.

For purposes of this book, the research of Bob Sutton (2017) and Ron Friedman (2014) has been very helpful in assisting us to more clearly understand both the healthy and toxic organizational cultures that we have experienced in our careers as educators.

Sutton (2017) is Professor of Organizational Behavior in the Stanford University Graduate School of Business (and Professor of Management Science and Engineering in their School of Engineering.) Sutton is a co-founder of the Center for Work, Technology, and Organization, which he co-directed from 1996 to 2006; and, he is also a co-founder of the Stanford Technology Ventures Program and the Hasso Plattner Institute of Design. Sutton is a New York Times best-selling author, known for his work on organizational culture and behavior. His books, articles, and presentations focus on changing organizations for the better, and he has written several books on the subject of toxic behavior in the workplace, including *The No Asshole Rule* (Sutton, 2010) and *The Asshole Survival Guide* (Sutton, 2017).

We have appreciated the candidness of his language and the direct way in which Dr. Sutton explores the nature and costs of toxic behavior in workplace environments. He argues that to create decent, people-friendly workplaces, leaders need to work actively to prevent toxic employee behaviors which create toxic organizations with inconsistent (or nonexistent) leadership ethics. One of his key perspectives is that toxic and abusive behavior is highly contagious, and it spreads and stays with employees long after an initial incident or exposure (Sutton, 2017). His view, and our experience, is that leaders, particularly very senior leaders, are often unaware of their impact on others. Sutton (2010, 2017) explains that the mixture of reduced self-monitoring by senior leaders and their increased visibility (or noticing of leader behavior by direct reports) makes even the smallest slights and insults highly toxic and potentially damaging for individual relationships and organizational reputation. We have certainly experienced this mindset in our work when attempting to discuss negative feedback or negative organizational data with particular educational leaders.

Ron Friedman (2014) is a social psychologist and author who specializes in human motivation. Although Dr. Friedman has served on the faculties of several American colleges and universities, he is known most for his contributions to various publications such as the *Harvard Business Review*, CNN, *Fast Company*, and *Psychology Today* and also for being the founder of ignite80, a consulting firm that designs leadership training programs. Friedman is the author of the best-selling book, *The Best Place to Work: The Art and Science of Creating an Extraordinary Workplace*, where he uses the research from the fields of motivation, creativity, behavioral economics, neuroscience, and management to describe what creates healthy workplaces (Friedman, 2014).

Friedman (2014) discusses the importance of building a workplace environment that fosters happiness, productivity, and creativity. He emphasizes the need for an organization-wide ethos to reduce fear of failure, suggesting that the way leaders frame their work and demonstrate their feelings can have a significant impact on how others approach their work. Friedman also highlights the importance of appropriately challenging employees and cultivating growth through intelligent risk-taking, suggesting that growth and innovation are negatively impacted when organizations try to avoid all types of failures and are "risk averse." These perspectives from Dr. Friedman clearly resonate with our work as school-based and district-based leaders.

Healthy Workplace Cultures

A healthy or collaborative workplace culture is a friendly place with the "right mix of pleasure, involvement, and organizational citizenship" (Rasool et al., 2021, p. 3). In a healthy workplace culture, staff well-being is a primary consideration, "Ultimately, employees [want to] feel included within the vision of the business and have a sense of belonging" (Spiers, 2007, p. 23). Effective collaboration and a positive team spirit are evident, and employees support each other. The goal is to create an inclusive culture where all levels/groups of employees feel a part of the organization; where each person is just as important as the next person; and all employees work toward common goals (Spiers, 2007).

Employee engagement is a concept often connected to workplace cultures. Employee engagement is described as a source of a mental and emotional connection between employees and their organization (Bakker & Albrecht, 2018). And, it aligns employees' professional and personal goals with the vision and mission of the organization, which typically increases the productivity of the employees and, as a result, creates positive organizational outcomes. An engaged employee works with a positive attitude, which contributes to the overall value and reputation of the organization. The Gallup organization (2024), which has studied employee engagement for many years, explains that employees want purpose and meaning from their work, and employees want to be known for what makes them unique; "This is what drives employee engagement" (para. 4). Gallup further suggests that employees want positive relationships, particularly with a leader who can coach and mentor them to the next level in their career, "This is who drives employee engagement" (para. 4). Gallup (2024) research indicates that 70% of the variance in engagement of individuals and teams *is determined solely by the leader. They explain that* employee engagement needs to be a leader's primary role responsibility because leaders are responsible for ensuring that employees know what work needs to be done, supporting and advocating for employees when necessary, and explaining how employee work connects to organizational success.

Friedman (2014) explains that, in order to develop a culture of positive employee engagement, organizations need to understand three key leadership "lessons." His first lesson is that psychological needs are at the heart of employee engagement. Employees are engaged in their work when they are provided "opportunities for them to experience autonomy, competence, and relatedness on a daily basis" (p. 270). Friedman's second lesson is that organizations are more successful when they consider the limits of mind and body. "Our brains have limited mental bandwidth...Instead of ignoring the body's limitations and insisting that employees power through periods of overload or low energy, organizations are far better off designing workspaces that allow employees to conserve their existing mental resources and offering them opportunities for restocking their energy supplies when they are running low" (p. 271). His third lesson is that integrating work and family life improves the quality of both, "In most organizations work-life balance is a myth...instead of pretending that work and personal time are separate, organizations are better off when they actively seek to blend the two worlds" (p. 273).

In order for employees to be engaged, satisfied, and productive in healthy and collaborative workplace cultures, the following leadership behaviors, principles, and processes are fundamental:

- Focus on human capital and onboard employees carefully.
- Listen carefully and communicate effectively.
- Set corporate goals collaboratively.
- Empower teams and nurture autonomy.
- Encourage creativity and intelligent learning from failure.
- Provide ongoing, strategic feedback and effective performance appraisal.
- Foster employee engagement, intrinsic motivation, and high morale.
- Model positive attitudes and organizational accomplishment.
- Design appropriate recognition and rewards.
- Design workplaces for the cognitive demands and psychological comfort of the work. (Friedman, 2014; Spiers, 2007; Sutton, 2010, 2017)

Toxic Workplace Cultures

We know that every employee has a "crappy day" or bad week at work from time to time. However, there is a significant difference between encountering a few aggravating incidents in your workplace and experiencing a toxic workplace. Particularly since the COVID-19 pandemic, a number of employees are no longer willing to tolerate toxic work cultures. In fact, a recent MIT Sloan study indicated that a toxic workplace is the number one reason for employee resignations (Sull et al., 2022). In addition to seeking a high salary, flexibility, and work-life balance, employees also want to feel psychologically safe at work. Kusy (2018) explained that toxic employees "are bullies, narcissists, manipulators, and control freaks; they're people who shame, humiliate, belittle, or take credit for the work of others" (p. 2). In a typical organization, Kusy posits that toxic employee behaviors impact an organizations' financial condition by up to 4% of total compensation costs—not to mention the impact of toxic behaviors on other employees' emotional well-being and team performance. In our experience as teachers and school-based and district leaders, toxic employees might be a colleague, your supervisor, or someone you (who as a leader) supervise.

When workplace cultures develop dysfunctional values and beliefs, negative traditions, and caustic ways of interacting, they have become "toxic cultures" (Mannix-McNamara et al., 2021). In current organizational development literature, the generally accepted characteristics of an unhealthy or toxic workplace culture are:

- Unethical behavior: This can include lying, making false promises, and racism or other types of discrimination. Such behaviors can lead to an unsafe and hostile work culture.
- Negative behaviors: These can include bullying, yelling, manipulating, belittling, and other forms of harassment. Employees may feel nervous to voice their concerns or share their opinions due to fear of rejection or reprimand.
- Passive aggressive behavior: This behavior may be demonstrated in various ways including non-constructive criticism, indirect or subtle prejudice such as microaggressions, or a supervisor who continuously talks about firing employees.
- Poor communication: Communication with employees may be ineffective or employees may feel like they are being lied to. This can lead to confusion and mistrust.
- Cliques and exclusion: The presence of cliques and the exclusion of certain employees can create a hostile and divisive work environment.
- Unrealistic workloads: Employees may be expected to handle excessive workloads, leading to stress and burnout.
- Unhealthy work boundaries: Toxic workplaces often encourage employees to prioritize work over personal life. This could involve expectations to stay late, to respond to emails after hours, or to work on weekends.

- Lack of respect and recognition: Employees may feel undervalued and disrespected, with their contributions not being recognized or appreciated. In some cases, their good work may be attributed to other employees or supervisors.
- Lack of transparency: In a toxic work environment, company values and beliefs are often obscure and rarely discussed or demonstrated. This lack of transparency can create distrust among employees.
- High employee turnover: A high turnover rate can be a distinct sign of a toxic workplace. Employees often leave such environments in search of a healthier work culture and better work-life balance. (Bortz, 2024; Forbes, 2021; HSI, 2024; McKinsey Health Institute, 2022; Sull et al., 2022; Sutton, 2010, 2012, 2017; TechTarget, 2024)

HEALTHY AND TOXIC SCHOOL CULTURES

Deal and Peterson (2010), aligned with Schein's view of organizational culture, explain that the school culture consists primarily of the underlying norms, values, and beliefs that teachers and administrators hold, particularly regarding teaching and learning. School culture has a profound effect on teacher professional learning, influencing attitudes toward spending time to improve instruction, motivation to attend workshops, and the [activities] people choose to participate in. As teachers learn how to work in alignment with the school's vision and values, a new set of relationship norms are created which are less to do with individuals seeking success for their own class, team, or department, but are now more to do with creating whole school success (Integrity Coaching, 2024a).

Deal and Peterson (2010) also indicate that in a school with a healthy workplace culture, there is strong camaraderie amongst all staff, with relationships built upon trust and understanding. "There's an informal network of heroes and heroines and an informal grapevine that passes along information about what's going on in the school ...[A] set of values that supports professional development of teachers, a sense of responsibility for student learning, and a positive, caring atmosphere" (Education World, 2024, para. 3). There is a shared sense of belonging, purpose, and a desire for the goals of the school to be achieved. No one is working only for themselves, no one is left out. All staff are made to feel welcome, and everyone is treated as a part of the team. "The professional bonds that exist amongst staff members are strong enough to weather the storms that can hit school communities" (Integrity Coaching, 2024a, para. 2).

In healthy school cultures, thoughtful risk-taking is commonplace. There is a freedom, a joy, and courage in which teachers and leaders go about their daily tasks. Creativity is fostered and individuals discover previously unidentified routes for fulfilling their potential. "A growth mindset is adopted by all and as such, mistakes are not seen as failure but as a source of learning and growth" (Integrity Coaching, 2024a, para. 4). By designing and trialing instructional strategies and initiatives and experimenting with new ways of classroom practice, teachers and leaders learn what works and what doesn't from both practical and theoretical perspectives.

Celebrating team and individual success is key to the development of a healthy school workplace culture. And, with this celebration, joy and laughter are present in everyday school life. "The school day provides everyone with opportunities to relax, reflect, to be themselves with colleagues and to have moments where they can be less serious" (Integrity Coaching, 2024a, para. 5). When this is the case, teachers and leaders feel more satisfied and passionate in their roles. Leaders and teachers working in a healthy school culture believe they have the ability to achieve their individual ambitions and the collective goals of their school community (Deal & Peterson, 2010).

Generally, in a healthy school culture, there is:

- A strong commitment to all students' learning.
- Shared goals and vision for teaching and learning.
- Collegiality and professional interactions.
- Continuous improvement and career-long professional learning.
- Encouragement for thoughtful risk taking.
- Celebration and humor. (Deal & Peterson, 2010; Education World, 2024; Integrity Coaching, 2024a)

Our perspective is that a toxic school culture is rarely caused by one individual's willful intent to create a toxic culture. Rather, it is a result of unethical or inappropriate behaviors and habits of teachers or school-based leaders that have been not appropriately addressed and have become negative school-wide norms:

Very often, initially, these behaviours and habits may not even be immediately obvious or even appear to be a huge problem. However, in a delicate school ecosystem where emotions are contagious and behaviours can easily impact one another; these limiting behaviours, attitudes or habits can gradually become endemic and slowly hinder both staff performance and the culture of the school. (Integrity Coaching, 2024b, para. 4–5)

In a toxic school culture, teacher interactions and relationships often involve conflict, staff members do not believe in the ability of the students to be successful, and there is generally a negative attitude to interactions with students and parents (Deal & Peterson, 2010). Also, individuals generally feel judged rather than supported. If a safe space does not exist for professional concerns to be expressed openly and honestly, without fear of judgment, then school cultures begin to develop that only serve to increase feelings of disengagement, mistrust, and isolation (Integrity Coaching, 2024b). And, behavior norms that develop are linked to self-preservation. Risk-taking and creativity very often are lost, and the dominant narrative in the school becomes "cover your ass" (CYA) or "play it safe." In those situations, teachers and school leaders typically do not believe in the possibility of realizing their goals for their students or for themselves.

Generally, in a toxic school culture:

- Communication is poor and hampers the development of trusting relationships.
- Collaboration is discouraged.
- Fear and judgment permeate most aspects of school life.
- Conflict and hostility are evident among staff.
- Students and parents are blamed for lack of achievement or progress. (Deal & Peterson, 2010; Integrity Coaching, 2024b; Mannix-McNamara et al., 2021)

From an organizational psychology view, Kusy (2018) has identified key strategies that leaders can use to offset toxic employee behaviors in order to improve team performance, restore personal well-being, and increase organizational productivity. In order to create a "culture of civility," Kusy's perspective is that leaders need to be teachers, teaching the values and strategies that the leader believes are most important to culture building to others throughout the organization—"and [leader] engagement is the key to dealing with toxic behaviors. It will create a village of everyday civility" (p. 6). Our experiences in schools and school districts in Canada and the United States—and also our professional interactions with teachers and educational leaders in these two countries—have reinforced the importance of leaders effectively (and swiftly) responding to toxic employees and to toxic school or school district culture.

From a review of current literature, next three subsections explore the possible impacts of toxic school and school district cultures on staff member wellness, employee development, and productivity and student learning outcomes—as well as parent and community perceptions of school system effectiveness. In the ethical leadership vignettes from teachers, principals and directors/superintendents which follow in Chaps. 6 and 7, these educators reflect on how their experiences with healthy or toxic workplace school and district cultures have impacted their work, student outcomes, and organizational credibility.

The Impact of Toxic School and School District Cultures on Employee Wellness, Productivity, and Professional Development

It is our experience that toxic school and school district cultures have significant impacts on employee wellness, productivity, and professional development in both Canada and the United States. These impacts may be seen in various aspects of staff members' professional lives, affecting both their mental and physical health, as well as their job performance and satisfaction.

One of the primary impacts of a toxic school culture is increased stress and anxiety among staff members. This can lead to teacher and principal burnout, currently a systemic problem across the United States and Canada, which can be exacerbated by a lack of support and an organizational culture that does not prioritize educator wellness (McMullen, 2023). Toxic school cultures generally have a detrimental impact on both the physical and mental health of staff members, often due to stress and anxiety associated with working in a toxic workplace environment. Effective teaching requires intensive investment of time and emotional, mental, and physical energy as teachers address the needs of their students. Chronic stress can impede day-to-day functioning and emotional balance; and, it is a risk factor for developing other mental health issues, such as clinical anxiety and depression. As would be expected, during the COVID-19 pandemic, a Canadian Teachers' Federation (CTF) survey indicated that 97% of teachers experienced increased physical, mental, and emotional workload and job demands during the 2020–21 school year (CTF, 2022). "This physically manifested through the cumulative exhaustion teachers experienced; in their acknowledgement of physical signs of stress like weight loss and sleeplessness, and hoarse voices from teaching through masks or stiffness from teaching online and working on screen for 12–14 hours a day" (p. 33). In a recent study completed by Canadian and America researchers in the province of British Columbia, teachers' job-related positive affect and intention to remain in the profession were primarily associated with their perceptions of support for mental health and well-being from their school systems, over and above the negative impacts of COVID-19 stressors and workload (Gadermann et al., 2023). Teachers' perceptions of support for their mental health and well-being were the most important predictors of workplace well-being. "Whether situated in the context of a pandemic, other global crisis…or in more 'normal' times, education systems can promote teachers' well-being by fostering strong, supportive school cultures, and positive relationships amongst all stakeholders" (p. 14).

Toxic school culture can lead to decreased staff morale and motivation, which can result in lower daily productivity, increased teacher absenteeism, and turnover.

According to a study by the Society for Human Resource Management (SHRM) exploring the impact of workplace culture on the well-being of employees, toxic workplaces have higher turnover rates than healthy workplaces (SHRM, 2019). This also leads to increased recruitment and training costs for the company. The report indicated that turnover due to toxic workplace culture may have cost organizations in the United States as much as $223 billion over the past five years. In our experience, the education and health sectors are often more impacted by absenteeism and turnover than other business sectors.

Toxic school cultures also lead to strained relationships among staff members, which can increase an already hostile work environment. Kusy (2018) explains that "toxic individuals often violate the organizational values, and we often don't hold them accountable to these values until it's too late, typically when leaders become exasperated and are at the point of firing them" (p. 3). However, terminating an employee is very difficult to do in school systems. Kusy also explains that because toxic employees can also be high performers, it is difficult to fire them unless they are held accountable to district values, "It takes a village, so it's said, to create a culture where toxic people don't get away with bad behavior" (p. 6). When behaviors of these toxic employees are viewed by other employees, particularly those who are working hard to contribute to a healthy culture, they create a sense of a "double standard" operating in the school. Also, when school leaders focus too much on district policy and procedures instead of empowering teachers to make decisions for themselves within their scope of practice, this can lead to power struggles and bullying within the school community. Teachers impacted by a toxic workplace culture with a toxic leader may also bring these negative effects home to family, friends, and significant others in the form of lashing out and/or a lack of communication (Snow et al., 2021).

Diminished collaborative professional learning and development is often one of the consequences of a toxic school culture. A negative culture can impact attitudes toward improving instruction and motivation to attend workshops and professional learning sessions, particularly if they occur within the school. Without a positive and collaborative school culture, efforts to encourage teachers to learn new pedagogical practices and implement them in their classrooms can be sporadic and weak. In a recent study of Irish teachers who had experienced a toxic school culture, participants were clear that seeking support from school leaders was not effective and that naming the poor behaviors was perceived to only make the situation worse (Mannix-McNamara et al., 2021). "There was a palpable sense of lack of agency in being able to stop the poor workplace behaviour that was having an adverse impact upon them…[however] several had embarked upon professional studies, such as postgraduate studies and were investing in their own sense of self" (p. 11). Interestingly, these teachers explained that engaging in their own personal and professional learning was key to repairing their self-esteem and sense of professional agency damaged by the toxic school culture.

The impacts of unethical leadership practices and toxic school cultures on staff member wellness in Canada and the United Stated are multifaceted and significant, affecting mental and physical health, job satisfaction, productivity, and the overall health of the school community (Sam, 2021). And in the literature, typically school leaders are perceived as having a role in the "facilitation or the mitigation of toxic culture, either by not recognising it or by actively colluding with it" (Mannix-McNamara et al., 2021, p. 11). It is critical for ethical school leaders to prioritize creating positive, supportive school cultures that promote the well-being of all staff members. "When there's a shared language around well-being, and structures and processes to minimize work-related stressors, then individual staff feel supported and part of positive community" (Naylor, 2019, para. 5)—all characteristics of a healthy school culture. This is certainly an area for further investigation.

The Impact of Toxic School and School District Cultures on Student Learning

For a number of years, researchers have indicated that higher achieving schools are those that demonstrate cultures that foster collaboration, empowerment, and engagement (Deal & Peterson, 2010)—indicators of a healthy school culture. In contrast, schools with toxic cultures where little collaboration exists were more likely to demonstrate poorer student academic achievement—the lack of teacher and leader collaboration a significant indicator of a toxic school culture. When teachers are excluded from the decision-making processes in a school, which is often typical of a toxic culture, it leaves teachers feeling that they have little authority, legitimacy, and agency. This exclusion can lead to a diminished quality of instruction for their students.

In terms of student impacts, researchers from several universities in Florida have also investigated whether school culture is related to student attendance and suspension rates (Ohlson et al., 2016). Teacher quality characteristics, elements of educational leadership, and components of a collaborative school culture were analyzed in their study. The data demonstrated that student outcomes are positively influenced when leaders work collaboratively, when teachers participate in professional growth, and when the school community unites in a common vision:

> A school faculty that works collectively and collaboratively will be able to share knowledge, skills, and practices needed to reduce suspensions. Then, a collaborative school will be able to work with families and community members to communicate and unify to ensure students are attending, and more importantly, learning. (p. 121)

Ohlson and colleagues' findings revealed that as teacher collaboration increased, student suspensions decreased significantly. From our school-based and district-based leadership work, we know that student achievement is impacted by poor student attendance and student suspensions.

Teachers play a central role in establishing a positive and responsive classroom environment that is conducive to social, emotional, and academic growth. Even prior to the COVID-19 pandemic, researchers from the University of British Columbia explored the link between classroom teachers' burnout levels and students' physiological stress responses (Oberle & Schonert-Reichl, 2016). The researchers were investigating the existence of a "burnout cascade" in which teachers' and students' stressful experiences are connected in a cyclic manner:

> Specifically, as teachers feel overworked while lacking support and resources, they increasingly experience occupational stress and tend to use fewer responsive and more reactive and punitive classroom management strategies. This leads to deterioration in classroom climate in which the emotional needs of students are not met. (p. 31)

The study identified that there was "stress contagion" between teachers and early adolescent students (in Grades 4 to 7) such that teachers who are suffering from feelings of emotional exhaustion had students with higher cortisol levels, which are linked to learning and mental health problems. This study highlights the importance of positive and nurturing student-teacher relationships and "emphasizes the importance of promoting well-being among teachers by offering the necessary support, resources, and professional development opportunities teachers may need" (p. 35)—characteristics of a healthy school culture.

Young people spend a large proportion of their waking time in school and questions are surfacing about how school culture might influence the overall health of young people. Research is beginning to connect toxic school cultures with short- and long-term health risks for students. In a recent American study by Boen et al. (2020), related to school culture and student health, findings reveal that across multiple measures of physiological functioning and psychological well-being, the social and structural characteristics of schools play an essential role in shaping health risk from adolescence through young adulthood—long after students left school. Although indicators of school-level violence had the strongest associations with health risk for students, perceptions of psychological safety and school social disconnectedness were also related to student health (Boen et al., 2020). When teachers are working in a toxic school culture where their psychological safety is a concern, they are not able to pay appropriate attention to the emotional needs of their students. "Teachers were not always available as a source of support, because they too often burned out from the physical and emotional toil of managing their own stress" (p. 2). In schools with toxic cultures, teacher turnover is often high, and students may not be able to develop the kind of relationships with adults that they needed to cope with and reduce their stress. This study suggests that school environments can serve as early life stressors in the lives of young people that unequally shape health trajectories and contribute to broader patterns of health inequality (Boen et al., 2020).

This is certainly another area for further investigation—uncovering both the academic and health impacts of toxic school workplace cultures on students.

The Impact of Toxic School and School District Cultures on Parent and Community Perceptions of School and School District Effectiveness

Parents' perceptions of school effectiveness are influenced by their positive connection with their school and their children's academic performance, as well as the classroom engagement and overall well-being of their children. When a school has a toxic culture, it often discourages parental involvement and can negatively impact students' academic performance (Schueler et al., 2017). This, in turn, can lead to parents perceiving the school as less effective. Lack of appropriate communication between leaders, teachers, and parents often leads to misunderstandings and tension building within the school community. This can lead to resentment and a lack of trust among parents and staff, ultimately damaging the school culture and reputation.

In addition, toxic school cultures also negatively impact the larger community's perception of the school district's effectiveness. For instance, a toxic culture often leads to hostile relations among staff, students, and parents, which can create a negative image of both the school and the district in the community (Deal & Peterson, 2010). In our experience, parents often have a more positive perception of the quality of the schools their children attend if the school leaders are visible and available; whereas schools whose leaders are viewed as aloof or "out of touch" are often perceived in a more negative light. In addition, parents generally have a more positive perception of the quality of the schools their children attend than other schools in the district—or the school district as a whole, whose senior leaders are often viewed as aloof and "out-of-touch."

And finally, this is certainly another area for further investigation—uncovering the impacts of school and school district cultures on parent and community perceptions of school and school district effectiveness.

School District Employee Engagement: A Canadian Vignette

For decades, schools and school districts in Canada have been expected by their ministries to gather feedback from students, parents, and staff members regarding the effectiveness of their schools and districts. In addition to measurements developed by the provinces, some school districts have engaged third-party companies to conduct surveys of employees regarding school and school district workplace culture. One of the principals that we have worked with described a school district which had been experiencing issues with employee disengagement for a number of years.

In an effort to improve employee engagement and their workplace culture, the director—supported by the executive leadership team and the board of trustees—hired a third-party company to meet with senior leaders to create an employee engagement survey, which would be completed by all employees in the organization. The results were to be disaggregated by service unit within the organization, but not at the school level. The survey results confirmed the lack of positive employee engagement and pointed to a negative workplace culture in the organization, with particularly negative employee perceptions of senior leaders. When the survey results were received, a number of like- and cross-role focus groups were created to assist the senior leaders to better understand the results and also to create actions to improve employee engagement and workplace culture. After the first survey, some district leaders attempted to publicly deflect the negative perceptions of their role by saying that employees who completed the survey were actually referring to school principals (not district leaders) when they responded to questions about senior leaders. Many principals were concerned that their credibility with their local school community was being damaged, and they complained to the executive leadership team. In a follow-up second survey, it was clarified that "senior leaders" referred to directors and superintendents in the district. When the same third-party company, conducted the second survey two years later, the results were even more negative, particularly related to directors and superintendents.

The principal explained that according to the executive summary of the second survey, which was provided to all employees, employee engagement in the organization had decreased from the first survey to an overall rating of approximately 50%. The report also highlighted that the lower engagement rating was impacted by the poor perception of senior leaders in the district. In the summary of the ten least positive results in the survey, the principal explained that four items were related to senior leaders:

- When employees were asked whether directors and superintendents made them feel motivated and positive about the future of the school district, there was only a 25% positive rating, down over 15 percentage points from the previous survey—and nearly 35 percentage points lower than other public sector Canada comparator organizations.
- In terms of employee confidence in directors and superintendents making good business decisions, again there was only a 25% positive rating, down nearly 15 percentage points from the first survey—and nearly 30 percentage points lower than comparator organizations.
- When employees were asked if they thought that directors and superintendents treated their employees as the organization's most important asset, the positive rating was just over 25%, down nearly 15 percentage points from the previous survey.
- In terms of directors and superintendents being accessible to employees, there was 30% positive rating, down 10 percentage points from the first survey.

A decision had been made by the executive leadership team not to disaggregate the survey results by individual school for both of the surveys, in an attempt to not create comparisons within the district, which the executive leadership team felt would be even more detrimental to the culture of the district. The principal explained that they "weren't sure if that was a blessing or a curse" because individual school leadership teams had no specific areas of strength or areas for improvement to target in their school-based work.

As a result of the further declining engagement results, the district planned to continue their work with the third-party company to clearly understand the results of the second survey and to work with employee groups and superintendent-led departments to attempt improvement in workplace culture. Then, the director who led this work retired; and, when the new director came to the district, the employee engagement process stopped.

Questions to Consider

- As a new school-based leader in this district, how would you approach this evidence of employee engagement? What indicators of a healthy workplace culture would you look for in your school? What would you consider as indicators of a toxic workplace culture in your school? Whom would you approach for assistance?

- As a new district leader in this school district, how would you approach this evidence of employee engagement? What indicators of a healthy workplace culture would you look for in your district? What might be indicators of a toxic workplace culture in your district? Whom would you approach for assistance?

The only thing of real importance that leaders do is create and manage culture.
—Edgar Schein, former Swiss American psychologist, professor, and organizational expert

References

Bakker, A., & Albrecht, S. (2018). Work engagement: Current trends. *Career Development International, 23*, 4–11. https://doi.org/10.1108/CDI-11-2017-0207

Boen, C., Kozlowski, K., & Tyson, K. (2020). "Toxic" schools? How school exposures during adolescence influence trajectories of health through young adulthood. *SSM Population Health, 11*, 1–13. https://doi.org/10.1016/j.ssmph.2020.100623

Bortz, D. (2024). *The hostile work environment checklist: How toxic is yours?* Monster. https://www.monster.com/career-advice/article/workplace-checklist-how-toxic-is-yours-hot-jobs

Canadian Teachers' Federation. (2022). *CTF/FCE pan-Canadian research report on teacher mental health.* https://www.ctf-fce.ca/ctf-fce-pan-canadian-research-report-on-teacher-mental-health/

Deal, T., & Peterson, K. (2010). *Shaping school culture: The heart of leadership.* Jossey-Bass.

Education World. (2024). *Is your school culture toxic or positive?* https://www.educationworld.com/a_admin/admin/admin275.shtml

Forbes Expert Panel. (2021). *Eight lesser-known red flags of a toxic work environment.* https://www.forbes.com/sites/theyec/2021/05/28/eight-lesser-known-red-flags-of-a-toxic-work-environment/?sh=3c7953e96189

Friedman, R. (2014). *The best place to work: The art and science of creating an extraordinary workplace*. Perigree.

Gadermann, A., Gagné Petteni, M., Molyneux, T., Warren, M., Thomson, K., Schonert-Reichl, K., Guhn, M., & Oberle, E. (2023). Teacher mental health and workplace well-being in a global crisis: Learning from the challenges and supports identified by teachers one year into the COVID-19 pandemic in British Columbia, Canada. *PLoS ONE, 18*(8), e0290230. https://doi.org/10.1371/journal.pone.0290230

Gallup. (2024). *What is employee engagement and how do you improve it*. https://www.gallup.com/workplace/285674/improve-employee-engagement-workplace.aspx

HSI. (2024). *10 signs of a toxic workplace: A checklist for managers*. https://hsi.com/blog/10-signs-of-a-toxic-workplace-a-checklist-for-managers

Integrity Coaching. (2024a). *5 characteristics of a positive school culture*. https://www.integritycoaching.co.uk/blog/relationships-school-culture/5-characteristics/

Integrity Coaching. (2024b). *3 signs of a toxic school culture*. https://www.integritycoaching.co.uk/blog/relationships-school-culture/3-signs-toxic-school-culture/

Kusy, M. (2018). Why I don't work here anymore: Leader beware. *Leader to Leader*, 1–6. https://www.mitchellkusy.com/wp-content/uploads/2018/06/Kusy-2018-Leader_to_Leader.pdf

Mannix-McNamara, P., Hickey, N., MacCurtain, S., & Blom, N. (2021). The dark side of school culture. *Societies, 11*(3), 1–19. https://doi.org/10.3390/soc11030087

McKinsey Health Institute. (2022). *Toxic workplace behavior and employee burnout: Fix one, fix both*. https://www.mckinsey.com/mhi/our-insights/toxic-workplace-behavior-and-employee-burnout-fix-one-fix-both

McMullen, J. (2023). *Stop the burnout: Enhancing support practices for principals*. [Organizational Improvement Plan]. Western University. https://ir.lib.uwo.ca/oip/366/

Naylor, C. (2019). *Staff well-being in schools: Some B.C. ideas*. Education Canada. https://www.edcan.ca/articles/staff-well-being-in-schools/

Oberle, E., & Schonert-Reichl, K. (2016). Stress contagion in the classroom: The link between classroom-teacher burnout and morning cortisol in elementary school students. *Social Science & Medicine, 159*, 30–37. https://doi.org/10.1016/j.socscimed.2016.04.031

Ohlson, M., Swanson, A., Adams-Manning, A., & Byrd, A. (2016). A culture of success: Examining school culture and student outcomes via a performance framework. *Journal of Education and Learning, 5*(1), 114–127. https://doi.org/10.5539/jel.v5n1p114

Rasool, S., Wang, M., Tang, M., Saeed, A., & Iqbal, J. (2021). How toxic workplace environment effects the employee engagement: The mediating role of organizational support and employee wellbeing. *International Journal of Environmental Research and Public Health, 18*(5), 1–17. https://doi.org/10.3390/ijerph18052294

Sam, C. H. (2021). What are the practices of unethical leaders? Exploring how teachers experience the "dark side" of administrative leadership. *Educational Management Administration & Leadership, 49*(2), 303–320. https://doi.org/10.1177/1741143219898480

Schein, E. (1985). *Organizational culture and leadership*. Jossey-Bass.

Schein, E. (2017). *Organizational culture and leadership* (5th ed.). Wiley.

Schueler, B., McIntyre, J., & Gehlbach, H. (2017). Measuring parent perceptions of family-school engagement: The development of new survey tools. *School Community Journal, 27*(2), 275–301. https://files.eric.ed.gov/fulltext/EJ1165635.pdf

Snow, N., Hickey, N., Blom, N., O'Mahony, L., & Mannix-McNamara, P. (2021). An exploration of leadership in post-primary schools: The emergence of toxic leadership. *Societies, 11*(2), 1–21. https://doi.org/10.3390/soc11020054

Society for Human Resource Management. (2019). *The high cost of a toxic workplace culture: How culture impacts the workforce—and the bottom line*. https://www.shrm.org/content/dam/en/shrm/research/SHRM-Culture-Report_2019.pdf

Society for Human Resource Management. (2023). *Understanding and developing organizational culture*. https://www.shrm.org/resourcesandtools/tools-and-samples/toolkits/pages/understanding-developing-organizational-culture.aspx

Spiers, C. (Winter, 2007). A healthy workplace culture: The key to sustainable success. *Management Services, 19*–23. https://www.carolespiersgroup.co.uk/pdfs/management-services-winter07.pdf

Sull, D., Sull, C., & Zweig, B. (2022). Toxic culture is driving the great resignation. *MIT Sloan Management Review*. https://sloanreview.mit.edu/article/toxic-culture-is-driving-the-great-resignation/

Sutton, R. (2010). *The no asshole rule: Building a civilized workplace and surviving one that isn't*. Grand Central Publishing.

Sutton, R. (2012). *Good boss, bad boss: How to be the best…and learn from the worst*. Business Plus.

Sutton, R. (2017). *The asshole survival guide: How to deal with people who treat you like dirt*. Houghton Mifflin Harcourt.

TechTarget. (2024). *11 signs of a toxic workplace culture*. https://www.techtarget.com/whatis/feature/Signs-of-toxic-workplace-culture

CHAPTER 3

The Influence of Trustees, School Boards, and the Ministry: "Tricky Politics?"

Abstract In this chapter, we consider the ethical leadership of the local governors of school systems and their ministries of education. We identify some of the influences of local and national politics on their particular leadership roles, as well as their potential impacts on the ethical leadership and workplace cultures in the school systems they oversee. At the end of each of the four country sections, there are reflective questions related to the role and impact of school boards and ministries. We also provide a vignette of an American school board member's ethical dilemma and questions for reader reflection. We have attempted to layer the information on leaders and ethics in Canada, the United States, Germany, and Finland in such a way that Chap. 3 information on the role of school board members and their governance frameworks also provides an overview of the education system in their countries. (It would be helpful to read this chapter before reading Chap. 4, which discusses district leaders in those countries, or Chap. 5, which focuses on principals in the four countries.)

Keywords Ethical school board leadership • National politics • Ministries of education • Local/municipal politics • Ethical school board governance • School trustee/board member codes of ethics

© The Author(s), under exclusive license to Springer Nature Switzerland AG 2024
B. Yee, D. Yee, *International Perspectives on Ethical Educational Leadership*, https://doi.org/10.1007/978-3-031-70839-8_3

> "Education is the most powerful weapon, which you can use to change the world."
> —Nelson Mandela, former South African President and activist

In this chapter, we consider the ethical leadership of the local governors of school systems and in their ministries of education. We identify some of the influences of local and national politics on their particular leadership roles, as well as their potential impacts on the ethical leadership and workplace cultures in the school systems they oversee. At the end of each of the four country sections, there are reflective questions related to the role and impact of school boards and ministries. We also provide a vignette of an American school board member's ethical dilemma and questions for reader reflection. As previously mentioned, we have attempted to layer the information on leaders and ethics in Canada, the United States, Germany, and Finland in such a way that this Chap. 3 information on the role of school board members and their governance frameworks also provides an overview of the education system in their countries. (It would be helpful to read this chapter before you read Chap. 4, which discusses district leaders in those countries, or Chap. 5, which focuses on principals in the four countries.)

In the international research and leadership consulting work that we have done, we have observed firsthand the impact of the organizational context on leadership mindsets and behaviors. In our experience with education ministries in Canada, the United States, Germany, and Finland, we know that the governance structures and contexts can be quite different across these four nations. In Canada and the United States, school boards are often very influential in their support for equity in student outcomes, principled treatment of employees, and ethical district leadership. We wondered about and wanted to further investigate the roles of school board trustees and ministries of education related to ethical leadership and workplace culture.

In each of the country sections that follow, we also provide an overview of typical governance and leadership structures set in their national cultural context which significantly impact ethical leadership in that setting. In our early experience as school-based leaders, we naively believed that the way our district and province operated was similar across all schools and school districts. We learned that we were wrong; some things were consistent across the province (and the nation), but many more things are different. It is our hope that leaders who have only worked in a Canadian or American school district might consider what they might learn from educational leaders and governance systems in other parts of our world. If nothing else, this is a provocation to ask more thoughtful, nuanced questions about ethical leadership. Chaps. 3, 4, and 5 in our book provide only a glimpse into the work of district and school-based leaders in Canada, the United States, Germany, and Finland—we know that it is not an exhaustive account.

The Influence of School Boards

In Canada and the United States, elected school board trustees have been a typical governance structure to allow for local control of public education, generally from the mid-1800s in both countries. According to the National School Boards Association (2024a), local control of American public education actually began in 1647, before the United States became an independent nation, when the Massachusetts Bay Colony passed a law requiring towns to establish and maintain schools.

Connecting to our inclusion of the German education system in this book, and this chapter specifically—Horace Mann who is also considered to be the first great advocate of public education in the United States was very impressed by the Prussian school system when he visited classrooms in Leipzig in 1843 on an education fact-finding mission (Miller, 2008). Mann, who was the Massachusetts Secretary of Education, did not support a school system based on social class like the one he observed in Britain. At that time in history, Prussian schools were considered a model for educational reform—a school system designed from the center with compulsory school attendance and teachers who were devoted to their students and trained at national institutes with the same care that went into training military officers. There was a national curriculum and system of assessment—as well as, age-grading and student literacy as a teaching focus. Back in Massachusetts, based on those Prussian reforms, Mann's vision for "common schools," which would be publicly funded and attended by all, represented an inspiring democratic improvement over the state's mixture of privately funded and sectarian schools, complete with their harsh approach to discipline. Mann encountered considerable resistance to his views on school reform—from clergymen who hated nonsectarian schools, to educators who condemned his pedagogy as not supportive of classroom authority and compliance, and to politicians who opposed the state board as an infringement of local educational authority (Cremin, 2024). But, Mann's views prevailed and made Massachusetts a model for taxpayer-funded public schools and state-sponsored teacher training in "normal schools." In the United States, there has historically been significant political tension regarding local versus state versus national control of education—with local control still dominating US discourse to this day. Eventually, the United States would have 130,000 school districts, many of them served by a one-room school. These little red schoolhouses, funded primarily through local property taxes, became the iconic symbols of democratic American learning (Miller, 2008).

Recently, the very divisive "right-wing versus left-wing" rhetoric (which has been growing in national and state/provincial political discourse in the United States and in Canada) is increasingly impacting school districts and schools. For example, recently one of our doctoral students, who is a school district superintendent, apologized for not being able to attend one of our class sessions because they were dealing with a parent protest which was happening prior to their school board meeting related to school district SOGI (Sexual Orientation and Gender Identity) policies. This is a clear example of the power of politics in educational governance—impacting trustees, superintendents, and principals.

In Canada and the United States, our experience has included working with a number of school boards, both being employed by the districts they governed and also consulting with district trustees and school senior leaders regarding their district improvement efforts. In Canada, it is quite typical that serving as a school trustee is the initial step to other civic or provincial political roles. While the majority of school trustees are focused on serving the best interests of students and parents in their districts, some clearly are not. Those trustees understand the power of the platform that being a school trustee provides them to advance personal interests and political agendas, particularly with school boards in large cities (Piscitelli et al., 2022). When those trustees are determined to control the direction of the school board and advance their own interests, it creates a very difficult dynamic for the superintendent or director to work within. Often the superintendent is drawn away from their focus on student learning and staff development to their own survival as the only employee of the divisive school board.

Campbell and Fullan (2019) have clearly described the value of school trustees and their unity of moral purpose for effective operation of school districts in the United States and Canada. Their book, *The Governance*

Core: School Boards, Superintendents, and Schools Working Together, outlines the importance of a governance mindset, a shared moral imperative, a unified and cohesive governance system, a commitment to system-wide coherence, and a focus on continuous improvement in the district. In the work Campbell and Fullan did with school boards, trustees described positive leaders as visionary, courageous, a listener, a consensus builder, wise, and ethical; and they described leaders who left negative legacies as arrogant, dominating, manipulative, dishonest, and unethical (p. 47).

ETHICAL SCHOOL BOARD LEADERSHIP IN THE UNITED STATES

The United States is a very complex environment for trustee and school board leadership. The tension between local control and federal accountability has been a defining characteristic of the United States across institutions, including education. In the last several decades, school reform efforts have continued to play out this tension, with a dominant paradigm of federal and state accountability emerging in the 1980s and the publication of the "A Nation at Risk" report (Lowenhaupt, 2021). "This shift toward standardization and accountability can be traced to an emerging discourse pinning the failures of the nation on the public education system, which was deemed underperforming and in need of substantial reform" (p. 178). Also, the school choice agenda has been prevalent in America for a number of years. Across the United States, an evolving school choice landscape reflects changes in the accessibility and desirability of an array of educational options, including traditional and nontraditional public schools, private schools, and homeschooling—with the impacts of the COVID-19 pandemic still yet to be quantified. Between 2000 and 2016, traditional public school, charter public school, and homeschool enrollment increased, while private school enrollment decreased. For example, traditional public school enrollment in Kindergarten to Grade 12 (K-12) increased to 47.3 million (1% increase), charter public school enrollment grew considerably to 3 million students (from 0.4 million), and the number of homeschooled students nearly doubled to 1.7 million. Private school enrollment fell 4%, to 5.8 million students (NCES, 2019).

American Students, School Boards, and Departments of Education

The U.S. Department of Education, which was created in 1979, is the agency of the federal government that establishes policy, administers, and coordinates most federal assistance to education, assisting the President in executing education policies for the nation and in implementing laws enacted by Congress (U.S. Department of Education, 2010). In each of the states there is a Department of Education (or Department of Public Instruction) led by a chief education officer, often called a State Superintendent of Public Instruction—but also called Commissioner of Education, Director of Education, or Secretary of Education, depending on the state. The Council of Chief State School Officers (CCSSO) is a nonpartisan, nationwide, nonprofit organization of these public officials who head departments of elementary and secondary education in the states, the District of Columbia, the Department of Defense Education Activity, the Bureau of Indian Education, and the five US extra-state jurisdictions. Their mission states, "We are committed to ensuring that all students participating in our public education system—regardless of background—graduate prepared for college, careers, and life" (Council of Chief State School Officers, 2024, para. 1). This organization provides a forum for connecting across the states to discuss policy issues and undertake projects of mutual interest, as well as a means to consult with and influence the federal Department of Education, focusing on "[driving] change to create equitable outcomes for all students" (para. 2).

Traditionally, local public school boards in the United States (also known as boards of education, school committees, school directors, or school trustees) are elected, or occasionally appointed, to be leaders and champions for public education in their states and communities (National School Boards Association, 2024a). Local school boards have responsibility for goal setting, policymaking, community involvement, and oversight of administrative aspects for their individual school districts. School boards derive their authority from the state. In compliance with state and federal laws, school boards establish policies and regulations by which their local schools are governed. Some of the key responsibilities of a school board include:

- Employing the superintendent
- Developing and adopting policies, curriculum, and the budget
- Overseeing facilities issues and

- Adopting collective bargaining agreements

Their most important responsibility is to work with their communities to improve student achievement in local public schools (National School Boards Association, 2024a).

Public education in the United States is supported by local, state, and federal government funds; and education funding for public schools can be a contentious issue. The proportions and sources of funding vary from state to state and even from district to district within the same state. Overall, about 48% of funding for public schools comes from the state. Local funding, that can come from property taxes and other local revenue sources, comprises more than 43% of the support provided to public education. The federal government contributes about 9% to public school budgets (National School Boards Association, 2024a). The National Association of School Boards (NSBA) is a national advocacy group for local school board authority—

> NSBA believes it is crucial for local school boards to maintain decision-making authority at the local level as well as accountability for high-quality educational services. The expansion of federal intrusion on public education in recent years has impacted local policymaking in ways that impose unnecessary rules, conditions and restrictions, as well as significant monetary costs, on local school governance. (National School Boards Association, 2024b, para. 1–2)

In the United States, charter schools are non-religious public schools operating under a contract, or "charter," that governs its operation. A key difference between charter public schools and traditional public schools is the regulatory freedom and autonomy that charters have from state and local rules (in terms of staffing, curriculum choices, and budget management). Charter schools account for 5% of the nation's public schools (National School Boards Association, 2024a).

In the United States, there are also private schools which have independent philosophies:

> each is driven by a unique mission. They are also independent in the way they are managed and financed; each is governed by an independent board of trustees and each is primarily supported through tuition payments and charitable contributions. They are accountable to their communities and are accredited by state-approved accrediting bodies. (National Association of Independent Schools, 2024, para. 2)

For statistical purposes, these private schools are generally grouped into the following categories: Catholic, other religious, and non-sectarian (not religiously affiliated). Catholic schools include parochial, diocesan, and private Catholic schools. The other religious category includes conservative Christian schools, schools that are affiliated with other denominations, and religious schools that are not affiliated with any specific denomination. Of American students enrolled in private K-12 schools, 36% were enrolled in Catholic schools, 13% were enrolled in conservative Christian schools, 10% were enrolled in affiliated religious schools, 16% were enrolled in unaffiliated religious schools, and 24% were enrolled in non-sectarian schools (National Center for Education Statistics, 2019). In fall 2019, (the latest year of report for private school data) about 4.7 million K-12 students were enrolled in private schools in the United States (National Center for Education Statistics, 2022).

Overall, 53.9 million K-12 students were enrolled in American public and private schools in fall 2019. Public school students made up 91% of total enrollment; and, private school students made up about 9% of the combined public and private enrollment in every year from fall 2009 to fall 2019 (National Center for Education Statistics, 2022).

Ethical Leadership Standards for American Trustees

Each state establishes the basic qualifications and procedures for becoming a candidate and running to be a trustee for the local public school board. No single school board trustee job description exists, and different school boards and teacher associations offer their individual opinions on the value and impact of the role.

Ethical leadership for school board trustees in the United States often involves adhering to a code of ethics. For example, the "Ethics for School Board Members" from the Texas Association of School Boards (TASB) (2024a) describes specifics of trustee behavior and mindset—"Equity in attitude, Trustworthiness in stewardship, Honor in conduct, Integrity of character, Commitment to service, and Student-centered focus" (para. 1–6). The TASB is explicit regarding ethical leadership in its "Leadership TASB" program of board development services, which examine best practices and research-based techniques for leading school improvement efforts through policy, collaboration, and community engagement. They articulate a specific program outcome related to ethical leadership, "model the ideal of ethical leadership by encouraging, empowering, and mentoring others to support the ongoing programs of LTASB" (Texas Association of School Boards, 2024b, para. 5).

The National Association of Independent Schools (NAIS) also provides principles of good practice for independent school trustees, which emphasize high standards and ethical behavior in key areas of operation of their one school or their network of schools (National Association of Independent Schools, 2024). Specific issues addressed include conflict of interest, confidentiality, commitment to equity and justice, and support for board decisions.

Some typical aspects of ethical leadership for school board trustees in the United States include:

- Educational welfare of all children: Promoting the best interests of student learning in the district as a whole and making decisions of terms of the academic success and welfare of all children, regardless of their ability, race, creed, sex, or social status (New Jersey Department of Education, 2024)
- Mission and community relevance: Ensuring that the mission of the school district/school is relevant and vital to the community it serves and monitoring the success of the district/school in fulfilling its mission (National Association of Independent Schools, 2017)
- Communication and engagement: Encouraging the free expression of all board members and seeking systematic and effective communications between the board, district/school leadership, staff members, students, and members of the community (Texas Association of School Boards, 2024b)
- Professional development and training: Participating in professional development, training, and board development retreats to enhance trustee understanding of ethical leadership and governance (Pennsylvania School Boards Association, 2024)
- Laws, rules, and regulations: Upholding and enforcing all laws, rules, and regulations pertaining to schools and advocating for desired change through ethical and legal procedures' processes (National Association of School Boards, 2024a)

By adhering to these principles and maintaining a strong ethical foundation, American school board trustees can support ethical leadership in their districts and ensure the best possible educational outcomes for all students. Ethical leadership is essential for school board trustees themselves in the United States as they are responsible for making and influencing decisions that significantly impact the educational welfare of students and the overall culture of the school district or school.

Tensions Between Local School Boards and State or Federal Departments of Education

In the United States, school board elections generally follow the complex political structures that are part of their national electoral system. *Ballotpedia* is an online encyclopedia that covers federal, state, and local politics, elections, and public policy in the United States. It is sponsored by the Lucy Burns Institute (LBI), a nonprofit organization named after an American suffragist and based in Middleton, Wisconsin; and in 2013, it began to provide data related to school board elections. (Their database is used by the public and a variety of "mainstream" media and educational institutions such as the *New York Times* and Harvard University.) With approximately 97% of local school board members elected, some 9000 school districts across 35 states held regular school board elections in 2023 (Ballotpedia, 2023). In the American system not all school board trustee seats are elected at the same time (called staggered elections), but seats are typically held for a three-year term. To give a sense of the complexity, some school board elections are held annually, some held every two years in odd-numbered years, or some combination of districts with annual or odd-year elections and districts with even-year elections (Ballotpedia, 2023). The language used is similar to federal election with "school board battleground elections" highlighted. Although most school board trustees are nonpartisan, some states allow elections to clearly identify school board candidates as Republican, Democratic, or independent—with candidates sometimes creating coalitions and being endorsed by politicians from the two major American parties.

Typically, in the United States, the state Governor or the state Superintendent or Director of the Education Department does not have authority to censure or remove school board members for unethical behavior. Similar to other levels of American government, school board "recalls" are the process of removing a member or members of a school board from office through a petitioned election, instead of during a regularly scheduled election. Between 2009 and 2022, Ballotpedia tracked an average of 34 recall efforts against an average of 80 school board members each year. In nearly all states that allow local recalls, the final decision of whether or not to keep a trustee in office is put to the voters at the ballot box. A total of 19.5% of the school board members included in the efforts faced recall elections, and 9.9% of school board members were removed from office (Ballotpedia, 2023).

The laws governing school board recalls differ from state to state. Bad behavior, mismanagement of funds, conflicts with district administrators or teachers, refusing to listen to their constituents, and violating state "open meetings laws" are some of the reasons listed on petitions seeking to recall school board members. Typically, petitioners must deliver documents to the city or county election office—and sometimes to the trustees they are seeking to recall as well. These documents usually include the reasons petitioners believe the trustee is unfit for office and initial signatures from supporters of a recall election. If a petition is approved, recall supporters must gather a set number of signatures from district residents to force the petition to a vote. Recalls and other investigations of behavior and effectiveness are very stressful for the trustees and the superintendent and senior leadership team in the school district. Trustee attention is drawn away from working to improve student outcomes and employee workplace satisfaction to justifying their behavior and saving their positions and credibility as elected officials.

Questions to Consider

- Thinking about the Shapiro and Stefkovich multiparadigm framework (2022), in what ways does the ethic of justice apply to the work of trustees and education department personnel in the United States?
- How does the ethic of community relate to the role of the American school trustee?
- In the American educational environment with complex political processes, a school choice agenda, and a long history of local authority, how are tensions between local school district trustees, state departments of education, and the federal department of education increased?
- Although most American school board trustees are bound by a code of conduct, what might be the key ethical leadership issues that they encounter in representing their communities?

Ethical School Board Leadership in Canada

For many years, the adage has been "When America sneezes, Canada catches a cold." This refers to the ripple effects that American actions on politics, policy, economics, and culture have for their northern neighbor. Certainly, there are many close connections between the American and Canadian educational systems, and numerous policies and strategies which began in the United States have been adopted or adapted in the Canadian educational environment.

School boards and elected school trustees (also called school in some provinces) have been partners with local communities and provincial governments as long as Canada has been a country. The school boards in both Quebec and Ontario were created in 1841, as part of the legislation uniting Upper and Lower Canada. The Canadian publicly funded, provincially controlled school system was prescribed in the British North America Act of 1867 and detailed in the various Education Acts or Public School Acts and regulations of the provinces (Wallin et al., 2021).

Canadian Students, School Boards, and Education Ministries

In Canada, education is the exclusive jurisdiction of provincial and territorial governments, and most school districts are governed by democratically elected school boards (CSBA, 2024a). There is no Canadian federal department or ministry of education, which would be considered similar to the US Department of Education. There is an association of Council of Ministers of Education (CMEC) which provides Education Minsters from the ten provinces and three territories, a forum to discuss policy issues and undertake projects of pan-Canadian interest, a means to consult with the federal government and other national education organizations; and an organization to represent the education interests of the provinces and territories internationally (Council of Ministers of Education, 2024).

Under the Canadian constitution, provincial governments decide what school boards do, how they get their money, and how much local autonomy they have, which is why school board trustees across Canada have somewhat different roles. Some of the key responsibilities of a school board in a Canadian context include:

- Setting and administering the annual budget;
- Hiring and promoting teachers and administrators through collective bargaining agreements;
- Developing school district policies;
- Building and modernizing schools; and,
- Purchasing resources and supplies.

Canadian school boards are a link between the local community and the provincial government:

> They act as navigators for families and the public when they have questions or concerns about their schools. They advocate for education funding and highlight the importance of equitable access to education regardless of where students live in their province. And above all, they care about students and the future of education. (CSBA, 2024c, para. 3)

Some provinces grant school boards the power to collect local property taxes, similar to the American system, while other provinces provide essentially all school board revenue from the education ministry, where all taxation from various cities and towns in the province is pooled. Where they do have the right to collect local taxes, school boards do have more control over how education dollars are spent in their communities. "While school boards have been a long-standing cornerstone in public education in Canada, they have evolved over the years in an attempt to better accommodate the needs of students, schools, and communities" (CSBA, 2024a, para. 4).

In Canada there are approximately 450 school boards/authorities and approximately 3500 school board trustees (CSBA, 2023). Each province establishes the basic qualifications and procedures for becoming a candidate for local school trustee through the School Act or Education Act. They are elected for four years in the same municipal election that elects city or town councilors (typically in October). As in the United States, no single school board trustee job description exists, and different school boards and teacher associations offer their individual opinions on the role. In an attempt to involve student voice in decision-making, since 1998, Ontario school boards that operate secondary schools have been required under the Ontario Education Act to appoint at least one "student trustee" to provide advice to the elected trustees (Wallin et al., 2021). These student trustees do not vote on board decisions or attend in-camera meetings.

For statistical purposes in Canada, students are described as attending public schools, attending private/independent schools, or being home schooled (Statistics Canada, 2022). Public Kindergarten to Grade 12 (K-12) schools are publicly funded schools that are operated by school boards or the province/territory; and, they may operate in the French language or have a religious affiliation. For example, in Alberta, "public" school districts have no religious affiliation, "separate" school districts are publicly funded with a focus on the Catholic religion, "francophone" school districts are publicly funded with French as the language of instruction and school district operation, and "charter" schools are also publicly funded. (Alberta is the only Canadian province that allows charter schools.)

Private/independent K-12 schools are operated, managed, and administered by private individuals and/or groups. All ten provinces allow independent schools. Five provinces provide government funding for independent schools—British Columbia, Alberta, Saskatchewan, Manitoba, and Quebec. The governments in Ontario and the four Atlantic provinces do not allow money to follow children to the school of their choice (Zwaagstra et al., 2023). The extent to which an independent school receives its funding from public or private sources depends on the province where it is located—ranging between 35 and 80% of public school per-student operating allocations. British Columbia has the highest level of enrollment in independent schools (13.2% of total enrollment), with Quebec following closely at 11.7% of students. New Brunswick maintains the lowest level of enrollment at independent schools (1%); and, all of the Atlantic Provinces record comparatively low levels of independent school enrollment.

Home-schooling is an alternative method of education in Canada that takes place outside public or private school environments. Parents have the primary responsibility of managing, delivering, and supervising their children's courses and programs of learning; they often are assisted by fee-for-service agreements with school districts or online educational course providers. In 2019–20, Alberta recorded the highest rate of students enrolled in home schooling at approximately 2% (Zwaagstra et al., 2023).

In addition, there are approximately 500 schools on First Nations reserves in Canada; these schools, in contrast, are the responsibility of the federal government.

In Canadian schools in 2021, approximately 5,000,000 students attended public schools, nearly 420,000 students attended private/independent schools, and approximately 84,000 students were home schooled (Statistics Canada, 2022).

Ethical Leadership Standards for Canadian Trustees

Similar to the United States, there is a national advocacy association for school boards, the Canadian School Boards Association—L'Association canadienne des commissions/conseils scolaires (CSBA-ACCCS). The mission of the CSBA (CSBA, 2024d) is to support member school boards from the various Canadian provinces and territories and to advocate for the collective interests of the provincial/territorial associations of school boards. A key focus is promotion of the value of democratically elected school boards. Although they describe themselves as an advocate, the CSBA is articulate regarding their "ambassador" role as equally important. "Therefore, as ambassadors, the CSBA Board of Directors and members must adhere to a strong Code of Conduct that supports the CSBA and its work" (CSBA, 2020, p. 1). Unlike the American NSBA which is silent (or not explicit) on the issue of ethical leadership, the CSBA is very clear about ethical leadership from all of its members, with a Code of Ethics policy document that indicates "The CSBA Code of Conduct requires all members to act ethically and with integrity, to promote diversity, respect and inclusion in all Board activities" (p. 1). The organization website is a repository of trustee governance and professional development resources created by the various provincial associations. CSBA is also concerned with ethical school board election processes and has supports available for local districts related to inclusion of traditionally "racialized" candidates, "To best support all students, we need to invite diverse and traditionally racialized candidates so that boards reflect all voices at the governance level, in addition to looking at governance practices to truly welcome candidates to actively participate" (CSBA, 2024b, para. 2). Because Canada has two official languages, English and French, the CSBA materials are available in both languages.

In each of the Canadian provinces and territories, there are provincial/territorial school board associations to provide additional support and advocacy for school boards in their province. There is general alignment between the provincial association and the local school boards, but local boards are able to focus on the particular needs of their communities. For example, the Ontario Public School Boards' Association (OPSBA) advocates for public education in Ontario. Their values statement indicates that they operate by the following guiding principles:

- Equity, diversity, and inclusion
- Truth and reconciliation
- Valuing student voice

- Quality and innovation
- Environmental stewardship, good governance, accountability, collaboration, and integrity (Ontario Public School Boards' Association, 2024).

This provincial association does not specifically mention ethical leadership, rather civil behavior; however, a focus on ethical leadership may be explicit at the local school board level. For example, in York Region District School Board (YRDSB) (2024) similar to other Ontario school boards, trustees are required by the Ministry of Education to establish an annual Multi-Year Strategic Plan (MYSP) to guide system direction for a four-year period. YRDSB indicates that the current strategic plan is a reflection of emergent priorities identified by their educational communities; and the trustees will focus on the priorities of well-being and mental health, equity and inclusivity, collaborative relationships, and ethical leadership.

Ethical leadership for school board trustees in Canada often involves adhering to a code of ethics—for example, in the Saskatchewan School Boards Association policy (SSBA) (2015). A number of the provincial associations work closely with their provincial government. For example in British Columbia, the British Columbia School Trustees Association (BCSTA) and the BC Ministry of Education and Child Care have collaborated to create a policy document to assist school boards in the review of their trustee code of conduct with criteria outlined to set a common approach and ensure BC boards can focus on their core responsibilities to deliver an educational program and to support safe and inclusive schools and workplaces. Related to ethical leadership, this document refers specifically to respectful workplaces and relationships with others (Government of British Columbia, 2023). Regarding healthy workplace cultures, in the York Region District School Board strategic plan, trustees prioritize fostering well-being and mental health in their district, and they indicate that they will "create safe, healthy, and inclusive learning and working environments" (York Region District School Board, 2024, para. 4).

As previously mentioned, Canadian trustees are expected to act ethically and with integrity and to promote diversity, respect, and inclusion. Similar to the United States, some typical aspects of ethical leadership for school board trustees in Canada include:

- Educational welfare of all children: Promoting the best interests of student learning in the district as a whole and making decisions of terms of the student achievement, equity, and well-being, inclusive of all abilities, races, cultures, genders, or social status (York Region District School Board, 2024)
- Mission and community relevance: Ensuring that the mission of the school district is relevant and vital to the community it serves and monitoring the success of the district/school in fulfilling its mission (Alberta Catholic School Trustees' Association, 2024)
- Communication and engagement: Encouraging the appropriate expression of all board members and seeking systematic and effective communications between the board, district/school leadership, staff members, students, and all members of the community including acceptable use of social media and incorporation of "plain language" accessible to the public (Government of British Columbia, 2023)
- Professional development and training: Participating in onboarding processes, professional development, and board development retreats to enhance their understanding of ethical leadership and governance, particularly related to Indigenous education (and the Truth and Reconciliation Commission's Calls to Action) and anti-racism initiatives (Canadian School Boards Association, 2024c)
- Legislation and regulations: Fulfilling legal responsibilities as set out in the School Act and under Common Law; Aligning with existing provincial and federal legislation and advocating for desired changes through ethical and legal procedures/processes (Ontario Public School Boards' Association, 2016).

By adhering to these principles and maintaining a strong ethical foundation, Canadian school board trustees/commissioners can support ethical leadership in their districts and ensure the best possible educational outcomes for all students. Ethical leadership is essential for school board trustees themselves in Canada as they are responsible for making and influencing decisions that significantly impact the educational welfare of students and the overall culture of the school district or school.

Tensions Between Local School Boards and Ministries of Education

Ministers of Education in Canadian provinces and territories have wide ranging authority including the power to investigate the operation and conduct of a school board. They are also able to disband a school board and then appoint an official trustee. Issues that would typically trigger an investigation include, if the board is in serious financial jeopardy, if there is non-compliance with the provincial Education/School Act, if there is poor performance of the duties of the board, if there is a risk to student achievement in the district, or if the board has failed to comply with a ministerial directive (Government of British Columbia, 2024).

As in the United States, there have been numerous discussions regarding the value and roles of local school boards, depending on the political landscape of the province. Over the past decade, the four Atlantic provinces have been involved in significant consolidation related to their local school boards (Wallin et al., 2021). Prince Edward Island school board elections for the English-language board (called the Public Schools Branch) were eliminated in 2011, and trustees were appointed by the minister; however, English-language board elections were reinstated in 2022. The French-language board continued to elect trustees during that time period. In 2012, New Brunswick merged and renamed 14 local school districts into seven regional ones based on language (Anglophone and Francophone), in an administrative cost saving measure. In 2013, Newfoundland and Labrador amalgamated all local school boards into one English-language board and one French-language board. In 2018, Nova Scotia dissolved its seven local English school boards and replaced them with a central Education Service Centre and provincial Advisory Council; the elected Francophone board remained intact. In 2020, the Quebec Government converted its 60 French Language School Boards to Education Service Centres replacing elected school trustees with an appointed 15-person Board of Directors for each Service Centre (Wallin et al., 2021). In Manitoba in 2022, legislation that was introduced to abolish school boards and replace them with a Provincial Educational Authority was very divisive and did not pass in the provincial legislature. Across Canada, the centralization of authority and the shift in local oversight by elected school trustees to centrally appointed officials have been significant developments. The tensions, consolidations, and reorganizations continue.

We have worked as employees for boards which have been investigated because of financial jeopardy and poor performance of the board. And, we have also worked for boards which have been disbanded by the provincial minister of education. Investigations by the ministry are very stressful for the trustees and also for the superintendent and senior leadership teams in the school districts. Trustee attention is drawn away from working to improve student outcomes and employee workplace satisfaction to justifying their behavior and saving their positions and credibility as elected officials.

Questions to Consider

- Thinking about the Shapiro and Stefkovich multiparadigm framework (2022), in what ways does the ethic of justice apply the work of Canadian school board members and education ministry personnel?
- How does the ethic of community relate to the role of the school trustee/commissioner?
- In the Canadian educational environment, where language rights in English and French were included in the British North America Act of 1867 (now known as the Constitution Act) and the role of the two official languages strengthened in the Canadian Charter of Rights and Freedoms in 1982, how are tensions between school trustees and ministries of education increased?
- Although most Canadian school board trustees are bound by a code of conduct, what might be the key ethical leadership issues that they encounter in representing their communities?

ETHICAL SCHOOL BOARD LEADERSHIP IN FINLAND

Ethical educational leadership in Finland is deeply rooted in the cultural and social foundations of the country. "Finland has undergone a profound economic and educational transformation in the past half-century and particularly since a major banking crisis pushed unemployment up to 18% and public debt over 60% of GDP in the early 1990s" (Hargreaves et al., 2007, p. 11). From being an isolated rural economy, Finland has transformed itself into a high performing economy. As a nation, Finland endured almost seven centuries of control by Sweden and Russia between which it remains sandwiched—and has achieved true independence only within the last three generations. "In the context of this historical legacy, and in the face of a harsh and demanding climate and northern geography, it is not surprising that one of the most popular Finnish sayings translates as 'It was long, and it was hard, but we did it!'" (p. 12). At the core of this country's success and sustainability is its ability to reconcile, harmonize, and integrate those elements that have divided other developed economies and societies—a prosperous, high performing economy and a socially just society (Hargreaves et al., 2007). It has generally been a positive outlier in the performance of its educational system, with highly trained teachers and excellent student outcomes on international measures such as Programme for International Student Assessment (PISA) assessments.

However, as Finnish society and its policies have adapted in the globalizing world with an increasingly diverse society influenced by immigration, uniquely "Finnish ways" have had to be developed in order to preserve and advance their nation.

> Finland has tried to develop itself by first attempting to cling to those values and policies that seem to be valuable and sustainable and then to change those policies that need to be altered in ways that do not destroy what is regarded as valuable and sustainable to maintain. (Risku et al., 2014, p. 33)

Technological creativity and competitiveness do not disconnect Finns from their past but link them to it in a cultural narrative of lifelong learning and societal development (Hargreaves et al., 2007). All this occurs within a strong welfare state that steers the economy and the educational system.

Finnish Students, School Boards, and the Education Ministry

From being a centrally planned and hierarchical system in the 1970s, the Finnish educational system was transformed, following the economic collapse of the early 1990s, into a highly decentralized system of governance with considerable decision-making power devolved to the country's trusted municipalities (Hargreaves et al., 2007). Decentralization has become a significant driver across national policy, and municipalities received autonomy in the Constitution of 1999 on how to organize themselves and their services. Public education is viewed as critical to the country's prosperity, and there is the high regard for educators who are seen as central to this cultural narrative. In a society with high taxation and relatively modest income differentials, teachers are paid well. "Working conditions and resources are supportive, schools are well-equipped, and like other Finnish professionals, teachers enjoy considerable trust and autonomy" (Hargreaves et al., 2007, p. 15). Teaching is highly competitive (with only approximately 10% of applicants to certain programs being successful) and attracts high performing secondary school graduates. In this sense, the high quality and performance of Finland's educational system cannot be separated from the clarity and broad consensus regarding the country's social vision.

In Finland, the education system is divided into three main tiers—basic education, upper secondary general or vocational education, and higher education. In terms of legislation, the Basic Education Act does not contain any rules or regulations as to how the administration and management of schools should be organized; instead, the administration of basic education schools is primarily under the regulations of the Local Government Act (European Commission, 2024). Each basic education school is required to have a principal who is responsible for its operations. Administration of upper secondary education is also under the legislation in the Local Government Act. Consequently, upper secondary school operation can be determined by the administrative regulations and standing orders of the local municipality, similar to basic education. Schools providing general upper secondary education must also always have a principal responsible for their operation.

The Finnish education system is organized at two levels. Education policy is the responsibility of the Ministry of Education and Culture; and, this ministry determines the general national objectives of basic education and general upper secondary education and also the allocation of the time to be used for instruction in different subjects (Risku et al., 2014). The Finnish National Agency for Education is responsible for the implementation of that policy, setting the national core curriculum and guidelines for schools (European Commission, 2024). This national curriculum determines overall policy direction and develops a broad curriculum framework—for instance, specifying a syllabus of 75 courses and 18 different subjects including 6 compulsory courses at the national level (Hargreaves et al., 2007). The local municipality is responsible for creating the final and more detailed local curriculum and a yearly work plan on the basis of the national guidelines. "Municipal school boards are thus not merely deciding on 'blueprints' of state policies, but have genuine autonomy and power in the local curriculum development" Risku et al., 2014, p. 34).

The public education system provides education free of charge as a universal right beginning in pre-primary, through basic education, and into higher education. Education is funded as part of the statutory government transfer system to local municipalities, joint municipal authorities, and private education providers. The amount (€/student) is calculated according to the unit price determined in advance for the subsequent year by the Ministry of Education and Culture. For basic education, the statutory government transfer covers 34% of the operating costs. For general upper secondary education, the transfer is 42% (Risku et al., 2014). The subsidies are paid directly to the local municipality and are not targeted for a particular purpose. The rest of the operating costs for schools remain with the local municipality to cover, and residents pay a municipal tax that is a form of income tax. Municipalities are also entitled to a share of the corporate tax revenue determined by Parliament (Government of Finland, 2022). There are no national standards or decrees for determining the student/teacher ratio, except for special needs classes in basic education. Again, local municipalities (and as a result, municipal school boards) have considerable autonomy in their decision-making. The municipalities also have the autonomy to delegate the decision-making power to the schools. Fundamentally, the responsibility of the local authorities is to offer all children living in their area (including those with mental or physical disabilities) an opportunity to learn according to their abilities (European Commission, 2024). At the heart of the human relationships that comprise Finland's educational system and society is a strong culture of trust, cooperation, and responsibility. Problems are typically solved through cooperation. Caring for children and for one another is a prime societal and professional value, especially for those individuals who have the greatest difficulty. "Educators at one school we visited explained that Finland performs well not by creating geniuses but by lifting up each child from the bottom" (Hargreaves et al., 2007, p. 15).

As of 2021, there were 309 municipalities in Finland, of which 107 were cities or towns. Sixteen municipalities were unilingually Swedish, while 33 were bilingual Finnish and Swedish. Four municipalities in northern Lapland had one or all of the three Sami languages spoken in Finland as an official language. In 2013, approximately 68% of the 320 municipalities had fewer than 10,000 people, and there were only nine cities with more than 100,000 inhabitants. About half of the population lived in municipalities, the sizes of which were between 10,000 and 100,000 (Risku et al., 2014, p. 36). There has been a heated political debate in Finland about reforming the municipality system over the past decade. Essentially, the number of small municipalities is considered to be detrimental to the provision of high-quality public services. As a result, there have been suggestions regarding nationally imposed mergers. In the typical Finnish manner of cooperation and problem-solving, during the period between 2005 and 2021, the number of municipalities was voluntarily reduced from 444 to 309. These municipalities have considerable power, "including allocating budgets between education, health and social services, designing and distributing curriculum specific to the schools and the municipality, determining the appointment criteria for principals, and conducting self evaluations" (Hargreaves et al., 2007, p. 19).

There are Finnish school boards, but their role and the role of school board members is somewhat different than what is typically understood in the United States or Canada. And, the concept of local board trustee does not directly apply in Finland. In a survey of school boards members, Risku et al. (2014) explained "It does not seem to be common in Finland that school board members represent individual schools as most of the respondents informed not to represent any school" (p. 40).

In addition to organizing instruction, each municipality is generally responsible for social welfare services for students. These services also include free school meals, free school health care, free dental care, and free services of student welfare officers and school psychologists. A local municipality must, in certain circumstances, organize other services such as transportation for pupils who need it (European Commission, 2024). At the school level, all schools have right to provide educational services according to their own administrative arrangements and visions, as long as the basic functions, determined by Finnish law, are carried out. There are no regulations governing class size, and the local municipalities and schools are free to determine how to group students. Also, it is typical that the principals recruit the staff members for their schools. The teachers have pedagogical autonomy and can decide their methods of teaching, as well as their textbooks and materials.

In 2022, the total number of students in basic education schools (also called comprehensive schools) was approximately 560,000 (Statistics Finland, 2022a). As the sizes of municipalities vary, so do also the number of students in basic education within the municipality. "The numbers varied between 8 and 46,185 [per municipality]. About 70% of municipalities had less than 1000 basic education pupils in their local provisions (Risku et al., 2014, p. 36.) Local municipalities assign students a place in a local school, but students are free to enroll in other schools. With approximately 45% of the schools having fewer than 100 pupils in 2014, recently Finns have been developing different approaches to school leadership distribution and cooperation to respond to pressures brought about by declining school enrollments and resources. With school mergers designed to increase enrollment in small schools, the numbers of basic education schools declined from 2644 in 2012 to 2039 in 2022 (Statistics Finland, 2022b):

> Measured by the average number of students, comprehensive schools are bigger than before…In 2010, an average of 360 pupils studied at Grades 1 to 9 schools, while the corresponding figure in 2019 was 464, i.e. a growth of 29 per cent in the average number of pupils. (para. 4)

A local municipality may also acquire the educational services required to fulfill its duties by purchasing them from other local municipalities, joint municipal authorities, or private education providers (European Commission, 2024). However, local municipalities are the main education providers for both basic and general upper secondary education in Finland. In 2009, almost all of the nearly 3100 basic education schools were municipal schools. Only 90 were private. Municipalities also maintain most of the general upper secondary schools. There were only a few that were maintained by private organizations (Risku et al., 2014, p. 35). Administration of a private school is regulated separately from the Basic Education Act. The development and organization of education is stipulated in the particular institutional regulations, which are adopted by the private school board (European Commission, 2024). Each private institution must also have a principal.

Leadership at municipal level is shared between professional administrators (e.g., the head of the educational section of the mayor's office) and elected politicians (e.g., the head of the municipal school board). Education is connected to broader local community affairs, "reinforced by the integration of educational administration into overall local administration including urban planning, local economic development, health and social care, housing or culture (Hargreaves et al., 2007, p. 20). Recently more autonomy, management tasks, and leadership roles have been transferred to the municipal and school levels.

Valuing lifelong learning in the way that characterizes all Nordic countries, Finland does not have a system of standardized testing or test-based accountability. It also does not have systems of competitive choice between schools, nor does it rank its schools in public performance rankings, which happens in Canada and other countries. The Finnish system is reflective and growth oriented and for those purposes the Ministry of Education and Culture (in collaboration with the Finnish Education Evaluation Council, Finnish Higher Education Evaluation Council, and the National

Board of Education) determines the general framework for national evaluation of their education system. The framework is based on the government platforms and five-year education and research plans, and it includes national, regional, and local levels. Municipalities do have the obligation to attend to national evaluation and to conduct a local self-evaluation. In a survey of Finnish school board members, Risku et al. (2014) found that board members were quite satisfied with the evaluation system. "They seem to think that evaluation reports compiled by the schools themselves give boards a good picture of the real quality of individual schools" (p. 43). The Hargreaves et al. study in 2007 explained, "In the words of school leadership training providers we met, 'all schools must be good enough and there is no reason to have elite schools'" (p. 20).

Ethical Leadership Standards for Finnish Board Members

In language related to individuals who hold elected office in Finnish school boards, they are referred to as "members" and not trustees. In terms of the role of Finnish school board members, as described in the Risku et al. (2014) survey, besides financial issues, school board members particularly emphasized the importance of developing schools and optimizing their school network, both long-term and short- term decision-making, strategic discussions, and results of school quality evaluations:

> School board members especially seem to acknowledge paying attention to marginalised youth, increasing financial needs of schools, rapid increases and decreases in student population, and school safety. Considerable attention also appears to be given to how staff is supported, management staff is recruited and both municipal and state statutes are abided by. (p. 42)

They regarded their work as meaningful for the development of the local schools and indicated they were respected by the local schools. They believed municipal executive boards took into consideration the views of the school boards. "In addition, they considered themselves to have the knowledge and skills to deal with school board issues, and the school boards to be able to influence decision-making in the executive board (p. 42).

Finnish school board members are generally people who have their own children in school or have another kind of natural connection to education. The gender distribution of school boards is fairly balanced (which is not always the case in Canadian school boards who generally have more women members), and there are people from various kinds of educational backgrounds, professions, and political parties. "School board members seem to consider the work of the boards strategic, meaningful, appreciated, and having a positive impact" (Risku et al., 2014, p. 45).

There is limited information related to ethical leadership expected of school board members in Finland or expected codes of conduct. In terms of more general political representation in national Finnish elections, a trustee model of political representation is understood—where the official makes their political judgments independently, based on what they think is best for "taking care of their voters." There is a stronger link between individual voters and their representatives and a somewhat weaker party unity in Finland compared with other Scandinavian countries (Bengtsson & Wass, 2010). In this study on Finnish political representation, over 90% of voters indicated that "representatives should act according to 'their own common sense' and 'regularly find out voters' opinions and act accordingly'" (p. 63). This independent style of representation, in line with the trustee model versus the delegate and resemblance normative models, was described as the most popular style of representation among the Finnish electorate. It could be assumed that those perspectives apply to the people who are elected to the municipal school boards.

In our work with Finnish principals and university professors, questions about leadership ethics were often met with quizzical looks and comments related to "why would we need to do that?" Similar to the views presented by Hargreaves et al. in the 2007 OECD report, we began to understand that in a Finnish education system (which is set in a Nordic welfare state system based on trust, collaborative problem-solving, and the expectation for both caring and highly expert educators) ethical leadership is assumed. Codes of conduct for school trustees "would not be necessary" because of the typical Finnish way of working, and of "being," in their educational system.

Questions to Consider

- How might the ethic of community apply the work of Finnish school board members and their Ministry of Education and Culture personnel?
- How does the ethic of care relate to the work of school board members?

- In the Finnish educational environment with a strong culture of trust, cooperation, and responsibility in a social welfare state, how might tensions between local school board members and the federal ministry of education be managed?
- What ethical leadership issues might Finnish school board members encounter in representing their communities?

Ethical School Board Leadership in Germany

In Germany, leadership in their education systems is certainly influenced by the country's cultural and social foundations—and history. Historically, Lutheranism had a strong influence on German culture, including its education, and in the 1500s Martin Luther advocated compulsory schooling so that all people would independently be able to read and interpret the Bible (Anweiler & Ifpling, 2024). The Prussian era marked the official beginning of German public education in 1763, when Frederick the Great of Prussia mandated regular school attendance for children ages 5 through 14. The denominational or confessional school remained the norm throughout Prussia during the nineteenth century reflecting the deep religious beliefs of the German people. The influence of the Nazi regime on the education system was also significant. After the Nazis came to power in 1933, they quickly passed new laws to make public education reflect and teach their nationalist and racial ideologies (Riché & Browning, 2024). After World War II, the Allied powers ensured that Nazi ideology was eliminated from the curriculum; and, they installed educational systems in their respective occupation zones that reflected their own belief systems. Currently, German school leaders generally regard themselves as closely connected to the teaching profession with limited decision-making authority, due in part to Germany's extensive bureaucratic traditions, requiring them to enforce regulations in up to four levels of school authority, from individual school to national levels (Huber et al., 2017). In recent years, Germany has been shifting from a culturally homogenous nation to a more pluralistic society shaped by immigration, which is also being reflected in its education system (Sliwka, 2010).

German Students, School Boards, and Education and Cultural Affairs Ministries of the Länder

For the most part, German public schools are operated jointly by the state (called the Länd) and local authorities or municipalities (called the *Kommunen*) with the federal government playing a very minor role in school governance and daily operation (European Commission, 2023). The Federal Ministry of Education and Research (*Bundesministerium für Bildung und Forschung*—BMBF) is responsible for the overall German education system with a focus on research and international cooperation, particularly across the European Union. Quite similar to Canada, there is also the Standing Conference of the Ministers of Education and Cultural Affairs of the Länder—a consortium of the ministers or senators of the federal states responsible for education and schooling, institutes of higher education and research, and cultural affairs. It provides a forum to discuss "educational, higher education, research and cultural policy issues of supraregional significance with the aim of forming a joint view and intention and of providing representation for common objectives" (Kultusminster Konferenz, 2024, para. 5). One of the key duties of the Standing Conference of the Ministers of Education and Cultural Affairs is to use consensus and cooperation as a vehicle for securing the highest achievable level of mobility for learners, students, teachers, and those involved in academic research (Kultusminster Konferenz, 2024). It is also charged with the tasks of helping create equal living conditions across Germany and of representing the joint interests of the federal states in the field of culture.

In German public schools, the cost of the teaching staff is borne by the Länd with other staff or material costs are borne by the local authority. The local authorities or administrative districts, which are responsible for the establishment and maintenance of schools and providing them with financing, are described as *Schulträger*, or school maintaining bodies (European Commission, 2023). Schools with a catchment area extending beyond the local authority area—for example, schools offering specialized education in artistic subjects or sport, *Fachschulen* (technical schools), and *sonderpädagogische Bildungseinrichtungen* (special education schools)— are in the majority of cases Länder schools which bear complete staffing and material costs. In some Länder, there are also Kommunen schools that are established by the local authorities; and, the costs of teaching staff and materials are provided solely by the Kommunen.

3 THE INFLUENCE OF TRUSTEES, SCHOOL BOARDS, AND THE MINISTRY... 71

The schooling system varies throughout Germany because each Länder makes determinations on its own educational policies. However, there is a typical basic grade, curriculum, and exit examination structure for German schools. After students complete their primary education (*Grundschule*), generally at ten years of age or at the end of Grade 4, there were four options (or courses of education) for secondary schooling:

- *Gymnasium* until Grade 12 or 13 (with *Abitur* as the exit exam, qualifying for university).
- *Realschule* until Grade 10 or 11 (with *Mittlere Reife* as the exit exam); students can then attend *Berufsfachschule* (full-time vocational schools) or *Fachoberschule* for two to three years, which combines vocational school and an apprenticeship. In some Länder there is *Regionalschule*, which is a combination of *Realschule* and *Hauptschule*. Students attend for either nine years, to obtain a qualification similar to the *Hauptschulabschluss*, or ten years, to get the *Mittlere Reife*.
- *Hauptschule* until Grade 9, with an exit exam called the *Hauptschulabschluss*. Afterward, students can attend vocational schools.
- *Gesamtschule* (or comprehensive school) which is a combination of the above, for five to eight years, with a different qualification for different durations—five years for the Hauptschulabschluss; if a student opts for the longer eight-year program, they can take the *Gymnasium Abitur* exam, qualifying for university.

The historic German tripartite system of education has been widely criticized for separating children along class lines at a very early age. In German Länder, a decision was made at the end of the fourth or sixth grade about whether a child is to continue onto the *Gymnasium*, the *Realschule*, or the *Hauptschule* (Sliwka, 2010). Since the very poor PISA results in 2000 with Germany ranking 21 out of 30 countries (Ochel, 2002), considerable energy has been placed on creating a more equitable education system particularly in their secondary schools—often focusing on the school improvement research from the United States and Canada. For example, starting in 2010, *Realschule* were formally abolished in Berlin and merged with *Hauptschule* and the old *Gesamtschule* to form new types of comprehensive schools, called Integrierte Gesamtschule, *Kooperative Gesamtschule*, or *Integrierte Sekundarschule*. In other Länder, the two courses of education of the *Hauptschule* and *Realschule* have been brought together under one educational and organizational umbrella: *Regelschule* (Thüringen), or *Regionalschule* (Schleswig-Holstein). The Gymnasium course of education is now also offered at schools combining three courses of education. For example, the three courses of education of *Hauptschule*, *Realschule*, and *Gymnasium* are offered at the following types of school: *Stadtteilschule* (Hamburg) or *Gemeinschaftsschule* (Baden-Württemberg, Saarland, Sachsen-Anhalt, Schleswig-Holstein, and Thüringen) (Kultusminster Konferenz, 2019).

Based on statistics from the German government, during the 2022–23 school year, there were 3,011,813 students in primary schools (Grades 1 to 4); 333,239 students in secondary general schools (Grades 5 to 10); 768,869 students in intermediate schools (Grades 5 to 10); 545,326 students in schools with various courses of education (Grades 5 to 10); 1,020,486 students in eight-year grammar schools (Grades 5 to 13); 1,256,523 students in nine-year grammar schools (Grades 5 to 13); 1,131,268 students in integrated comprehensive schools; 88,256 students in Free Waldorf schools (Grades 1 to 13); and 191,209 students in special schools (Grades 1 to 13) (Destatis, 2023).

Länder schools are free to attend. However, parents can also choose one of many fee-paying private schools (*Ersatzschulen* or *Ergänzungsschulen*). Article 7 of the German Constitution guarantees the right to establish private schools. This article belongs to the first part of the German Basic Law, which defines civil and human rights (Government of Germany, 2024). This unusual protection of private schools is thought to have been implemented to protect the education system from a second *Gleichschaltung*, which refers to when the Nazi party established a system of totalitarian control and coordination over all aspects of German economy and society (Riché & Browning, 2024).

Ersatzschulen (substitute schools) are primary or secondary schools which are run by private individuals, private organizations, or religious groups. These schools offer the same types of diplomas as in public schools and may offer the German *Abitur*. *Ersatzschulen*, like their Länder-run counterparts, are subjected to basic government standards, such as minimum required qualifications for teachers and pay grades. An *Ersatzschule* must have at least the same academic standards as those of a state school and Article 7 forbids the segregation of pupils based on socioeconomic status (Gellert & Ritter, 1985). As a result, most *Ersatzschulen* have very low tuition fees compared to private schools in most other Western

European countries; scholarships are also often available. Because it is not possible to finance these schools with such low tuition fees, private schools are subsidized with public funds, and some students attend private schools through welfare subsidies. This is often the case if a student is considered to be a "child at risk," such as students who have learning disabilities, special needs, or come from dysfunctional home environments.

International schools would typically be categorized as *Ergänzungsschulen* (supplementary schools) (Gellert & Ritter, 1985). Most of these schools are in bigger cities where there is a larger international or "expat" population. They tend to have a more multicultural mix of pupils than Länder schools and teach mainly in English, although some schools are bilingual (with German, French, Italian, and Spanish the most common non-English languages). These schools tend to follow slightly different international curriculums—for example, in International Baccalaureate (IB) schools. Most schools are day schools, although some offer boarding for students. Religious schools and method schools (such as *Waldorfschule or Montessori* schools) can also be found. In Germany, international schools are generally affiliated with the Association of German International Schools (AGIS) or are accredited by either the Council of International Schools (CIS) or the New England Association of Schools and Colleges (NEASC). Some international schools may offer the German *Abitur*. In 2017 approximately 750,600 children, or 9% of German students, attended private or international schools (Deutsche Welle, 2018).

Home schooling for pedagogical or religious reasons is not allowed in Germany. Obligatory schooling has been part of German law continuously since 1919 and is enshrined in several state constitutions as well (Deutsche Welle, 2019). There are different interpretations as to the reason, but generally it has to do with the importance German society places on children's rights (Bundesregierung, 2021). The exceptions are for severe illnesses, the children of diplomats, and in rare instances for working children, such as child actors. There are only between 500 and 1000 cases of parents homeschooling their children across Germany.

Ethical Leadership Standards for German Conferences

Local school boards or school board trustees, like those operating in the United States and Canada, do not have a direct equivalent in the German education system. The German educational system has a complex system of laws and processes for participation of teachers, students, parents, and communities in the development and operation of its schools.

In German education system, the term "conference" is frequently used to describe a group that has a formal role in educational decision-making—for example, teachers' conferences (*Lehrerkonferenz*) which involve all teachers in a school, meeting in small grade or department groups or as a whole school group. In the full teacher conference, where all teachers meet, it is generally the principal who presides over the conference and is responsible for the implementation of any decisions. In several Länder, parents' (and sometimes students') representatives have a right to make their views known and take part in the deliberations of the teachers' conference. They are not generally allowed to take part in discussions and decisions on what marks to award in certificates or whether pupils should or should not be moved up to the next school grade (European Commission, 2023). In some Länder, parents' and students' representatives do have an advisory vote in teachers' conferences—deliberating on certificates and on whether or not pupils should be moved up to the next grade.

Besides the teachers' conference, the school conference (*Schulkonferenz*) exists as an additional body governing cooperation between the principal, teachers, pupils, and parents—as well as any external cooperation partners. It is constituted in different ways in the various Länder. Sometimes teachers, parents, and students are represented in equal numbers in the school conference; and, sometimes teachers and/or parents are more strongly represented (European Commission, 2023). The school conference is chaired either by the principal or by a member elected by the school conference. School conferences have different rights to participation and consultation depending on the Länder. The Länder Education Acts also contain different sets of objectives for the school conferences, but these do not represent "hard and fast" regulations. Typically, the school conference is involved in school regulations and disciplinary rules, allocation of classrooms, school transportation, safety on school premises, and organization of events outside of the school which are under school supervision (e.g., school partnerships, stays at residential facilities in the country, or visits to museums and businesses/factories.)

In some Länder, similar to a school board in Canada or the United States, the school conference also discusses and approves/rejects the organization of the school in its present form, the relocation or merger with another school, and school construction projects. Also, corrective and disciplinary measures in conflict situations and counselling for parents and pupils may be dealt with (European Commission, 2023). Finally in some Länder, the school conference has a say in the selection of the principal—from the right to propose a principal to the right to reject a particular choice for principal. For legal reasons, however, it is the school's supervisory authority that formally appoints the principal.

Regulated Parent Participation

The Länder is fundamentally responsible for the schooling of children under Article 7, paragraph 1 of the Basic Law of the German constitution. However, the Länder's right to regulate the education of children at school is limited by parental rights to bring up their children. Parents exercise their rights individually and collectively through parents' groups, as well as their representatives on other consulting and decision-making bodies at schools. The rights of parents of primary school students do not fundamentally differ from those afforded parents of secondary school students who have not yet reached their majority age of 18.

Each of the Länder has developed its own approach to parent participation in schools based on the constitutions of the Länder and in their Education Acts (European Commission, 2023). It is typical that parents have an opportunity to make their views heard at two levels, the lower level being the individual class level (in bodies called *Klassenelternversammlung*) and the upper level being the school as a whole (in the *Schulelternbeirat*). In addition to the opportunities for parent participation through the various school conferences, there are also General Parent's Councils (*Gesamtelternbeirat*—GEB) which are usually arranged at the town or city level. The GEB consists of a chair and board members who are usually elected annually. As a rule, a GEB consists of the two chairmen of the parents' councils of each public school within the school authority. The school parent councils can also send special delegates as members. Any parent can put their name forward for election as long as they are able to speak and understand German at a conversational level. The parents' council chairs of privately run schools can also become members of the General Parents' Council if they meet the same requirements for their election as those of Länder-run schools. The main purpose of the GEB is to represent parent interests, to advise and inform parents on key issues, and act as intermediaries on problems that arise. These GEBs meet at regular intervals, typically quarterly or annually.

At a higher level, there are also regional parents' councils at the level of the local authority, town, or district and representative bodies at the Länder level (*Landeselternbeirat*), sometimes organized according to the different school types. Finally, the representative bodies combine to form a single Federal Parents' Council (*Bundeselternrat*—BER) at national level, providing a forum to inform parents on developments in the field of education policy and to advise parents on school-related issues. As part of its transnational tasks, the BER maintains close contact with ministries, institutions, and associations in order to promote the educational mission of the schools and to protect the rights of parents in accordance with Article 6 of the Basic Law (Bundeselternrat, 2024).

Regulated Student Participation

The Länder Education Acts and school participation laws recognize students' basic right to participation, and these laws regulate the makeup and responsibilities of the students' representative body. Students elect representatives from their grade or year groups to look after their interests in accordance with principles of representation in each Länder. Students' representatives make up the school parliament (*Schülerparlament*). This body elects one or more student spokespersons for the whole school (European Commission, 2023). In some Länder, the student representatives are elected directly by all students. At local authority (*Kommunen*), town, or district level, students are also organized into other student parliaments—and at Länder level into Länder student councils (*Landesschülerrat*). The principal and the school supervisory authorities usually are not allowed to influence the choice of student representatives.

As well as the student parliaments, Länder Education Acts or school constitution acts also provide for general assemblies of students (*Schülervollversammlungen*) either from the entire school or from different levels of the school, where it is intended that all students exchange opinions and hold discussions. From an ethical leadership perspective, it is clearly important throughout German education systems that students have a representative voice in decisions about their education.

In our work with German principals and university professors, our questions about leadership ethics related to school and district governance were often met with responses related to the laws and regulations of the school authority or Länder in their very highly structured system.

Questions to Consider

- How might the ethic of community apply the work of parent councils, Länder ministries, and the federal Ministry of Education and Culture?
- How do the ethics of care or justice relate to the work of parents who are members of their teacher conferences or school conferences?
- In the German educational environment with a culture of regulations and laws governing interactions, how might tensions between individual parents and the Länder ministries be managed?
- What ethical leadership issues might German parents encounter in representing their families and their school communities?

THE ETHICAL DILEMMA OF AN AMERICAN SCHOOL BOARD MEMBER

Board members, whether elected or appointed, generally have a strong desire to serve the schools in their communities, often ones their children attend or have attended. It is the belief that they can make a difference, support the good work already happening in the district, and bring about necessary improvements that drive their commitment as a board member. Challenges arise when board members, who because of their work have a thorough understanding of what is going on in the schools in their district, come to know of principal leadership practices that conflict with the board member's values. One American school board member describes their ethical dilemma.

Early into my appointment as a board member, I was approached by other members, indicating their grave concern about a culturally inappropriate and insensitive musical performance that was a long-standing tradition at the school. They indicated that for years they had shared their concerns with the principal and other board members, to no avail. This was an issue I felt strongly about, and so I decided to approach the principal to see if I could bring about what I thought would be an easy change. I soon realized why the other board members had been so frustrated and began to see why some members of the staff felt they had no voice in the educational programming at the school. A conversation ensued at a board meeting where I learned this had long been an issue and the board had repeatedly decided that it was not something they wanted to pursue. In their words, "we will just wait for the principal to retire." As a voluntary board member, and with the belief that the boards I serve on are a reflection of my own values, morals, and ethics, I made the difficult decision to resign.

Questions to Consider

- Thinking about the Shapiro and Stefkovich multiparadigm framework (2022), how does the ethic of justice relate to the board member's leadership dilemma?
- How does the ethic of care apply to this situation?
- Which of the signs of a healthy workplace culture or toxic workplace culture were evident in this leadership vignette?

The function of education is to teach one to think intensively and to think critically. Intelligence plus character--that is the goal of true education.
—Martin Luther King, Jr, former American minister, activist, and philosopher

References

Alberta Catholic School Trustees' Association. (2024). *About ACSTA*. https://www.acsta.ab.ca/about-us/about-acsta

Anweiler, O., & Ifpling, H.-J. (2024). Education: Luther and the German Reformation. *Encyclopædia Britannica*. https://www.britannica.com/topic/education/Luther-and-the-German-Reformation

Ballotpedia. (2023). *School boards: Examining K-12 education—policies and politics*. https://ballotpedia.org/School_board_elections,_2023

Bengtsson, A., & Wass, H. (2010). Styles of political representation: What do voters expect? *Journal of Elections, Public Opinion and Parties, 20*(1), 55–81. https://doi.org/10.1080/17457280903450724

Bundeselternrat. (2024). Federal parents' council. https://www.bundeselternrat.de/home/der-ber.html

Bundesregierung. (2021). Children's rights to be enshrined in German Basic Law. https://www.bundesregierung.de/breg-en/service/archive/rights-of-child-in-basic-law-1841338

Campbell, D., & Fullan, M. (2019). *The governance core: School boards, superintendents and schools working together*. Corwin.

Canadian School Boards Association. (2020). *Code of conduct*. https://www.cdnsba.org/wp-content/uploads/2021/06/1.2-Code-of-Conduct-Google-Docs.pdf

Canadian School Boards Association. (2023). *Annual report 2022–23*. https://www.cdnsba.org/flipbook/2023-annual-report/?page=1

Canadian School Boards Association. (2024a). *Public education in Canada*. https://www.cdnsba.org/public-education-in-canada/

Canadian School Boards Association. (2024b). *School board elections*. https://www.cdnsba.org/school-board-elections/

Canadian School Boards Association. (2024c). *Why do school boards matter*. https://www.cdnsba.org/why-do-school-boards-matter/

Canadian School Boards Association. (2024d). *About us.*. https://www.cdnsba.org/about-us/

Council of Chief State School Officers. (2024). *About us*. https://ccsso.org/about

Council of Ministers of Education. (2024). *Council of Ministers of Education, Canada*. https://www.cmec.ca/11/About_Us.html

Cremin, L. A. (2024). *Horace Mann. Encyclopædia Britannica*. https://www.britannica.com/biography/Horace-Mann

Destatis. (2023). *Pupils: Germany, school year, sex, type of school, year groups*. https://www-genesis.destatis.de/genesis/online?language=en&sequenz=tabelleErgebnis&selectionname=21111-0002#abreadcrumb

Deutsche Welle. (2018). *Private schools: Why does Germany allow them?* https://www.dw.com/en/private-schools-why-does-germany-allow-them/a-46775899

Deutsche Welle. (2019). *European court rules against German homeschooling family*. https://www.dw.com/en/european-court-rules-against-german-homeschooling-family/a-47021333#:~:text=Homeschooling%20has%20been%20illegal%20in%20Germany%20since%201919.&text=The%20European%20Court%20of%20Human,that%20is%20illegal%20in%20Germany

European Commission. (2023). *National education systems—Germany: Administration and governance*. https://eurydice.eacea.ec.europa.eu/national-education-systems/germany/administration-and-governance-local-andor-institutional-level

European Commission. (2024). *National education systems—Finland: Administration and governance*. https://eurydice.eacea.ec.europa.eu/national-education-systems/finland/administration-and-governance-local-andor-institutional-level

Gellert, C., & Ritter, R. (1985). The private school system of the Federal Republic of Germany. *European Journal of Education, 20*(4), 339–349. https://doi.org/10.2307/1503338

Government of British Columbia. (2023). *School trustees' codes of conduct: Provincial criteria guidelines.* http://www.bced.gov.bc.ca/bulletin/20230602/criteria-guidelines%2D%2D-may-25.pdf

Government of British Columbia. (2024). *School act.* https://www.bclaws.gov.bc.ca/civix/document/id/complete/statreg/96412_00_multi

Government of Finland. (2022). *Municipalities and local government.* https://www.suomi.fi/citizen/rights-and-obligations/digital-support-and-administrative-services/guide/how-finlands-public-administration-works/municipalities-and-local-government

Government of Germany. (2024). *Basic law for the Federal Republic of Germany, Article 7.* https://www.gesetze-im-internet.de/gg/art_7.html

Hargreaves, H., Gabor, H., & Pont, B. (2007). *School leadership for systemic improvement in Finland: A case study report for the OECD activity improving school leadership.* https://www.oecd.org/education/school/39928629.pdf

Huber, S., Tulowitzki, P., & Hameyer, U. (2017). Curriculum and School Leadership—Adjusting School Leadership to Curriculum. In M. Uljens & R. Ylimaki (Eds.), *Bridging educational leadership, curriculum theory and didaktik. Educational governance research* (Vol. 5, pp. 309–332). Springer. https://doi.org/10.1007/978-3-319-58650-2_9

Kultusminster Konferenz. (2019). *Basic structure of the education system in the Federal Republic of Germany* https://www.kmk.org/fileadmin/Dateien/pdf/Dokumentation/en_2019.pdf

Kultusminster Konferenz. (2024). *The Standing Conference of the Ministers of Education and Cultural Affairs (KMK).* https://www.kmk.org/kmk/information-in-english/standing-conference.html

Lowenhaupt, R. (2021). School leadership in the United States: Evolving responsibilities in times of change. In R. Normand, L. Moos, M. Liu, & P. Tulowitzki (Eds.), *The cultural and social foundations of educational leadership. Educational governance research,* vol 16. Springer. https://doi.org/10.1007/978-3-030-74497-7_10

Miller, M. (2008). First, kill all the school boards: A modest proposal to fix the schools. *The Atlantic.* https://www.theatlantic.com/magazine/archive/2008/01/first-kill-all-the-school-boards/306579/

National Association of Independent Schools. (2017). *NAIS principals of good practice:Independentschooltrustees.*https://www.nais.org/getmedia/a1c88f3d-79dd-4519-9a79-708ac37bb4e6/NAIS_PGP_ISTrustees_2017.pdf

National Association of Independent Schools. (2024). *What is NAIS.* https://www.nais.org/about/about-nais/

National Center for Education Statistics. (2019). *School choice: Summary.* https://nces.ed.gov/programs/schoolchoice/summary.asp

National Center for Education Statistics. (2022). *Private school enrollment.* https://nces.ed.gov/programs/coe/indicator/cgc

National School Boards Association. (2024a). *Public education FAQ.* https://www.nsba.org/About/Public-Education-FAQ

National School Boards Association. (2024b). *Local school board governance and flexibility.* https://www.nsba.org/advocacy/federal-legislative-priorities/local-school-board-governance-and-flexibility

New Jersey Department of Education. (2024). *Code of ethics for school board members.* https://www.nj.gov/education/ethics/coe.shtml

Ochel, W. (2002). *Results of PISA 2000: The case of Germany.* https://www.ifo.de/DocDL/Forum302-dice.pdf

Ontario Public School Boards' Association. (2016). *OPSBA board of director code of conduct policy.* https://www.opsba.org/wp-content/uploads/2021/04/OPSBA-BOD-Code-of-Conduct-Policy.pdf

Ontario Public School Boards' Association. (2024). *Mission, vision, and values.* https://www.opsba.org/about-us/mission-vision-and-values/

Pennsylvania School Boards Association. (2024). *Principles for governance and school leadership.* https://www.psba.org/principles-for-governance-and-leadership/#:~:text=Pennsylvania%20school%20boards%20are%20committed,advocate%20earnestly%20and%20govern%20effectively.

Piscitelli, A., Perrella, A., & Payler, A. (2022). Public expectations of school board trustees. *Canadian Journal of Educational Administration and Policy, 198,* 19–34. https://doi.org/10.7202/1086425ar

Riché, P., & Browning, R. (2024). *Education: Nazi and post-war Germany.* Encyclopædia Britannica. https://www.britannica.com/topic/education/Nazi-Germany

Risku, M., Kanervio, P., & Pulkkinen, S. (2014). School boards in Finland. In L. Moos & J. Paulsen (Eds.), *School boards in the governance process: Educational governance research* (Vol. 1, pp. 31–48). Springer. https://doi.org/10.1007/978-3-319-05494-0_3

Saskatchewan School Boards Association. (2015). *Saskatchewan School Boards Association code of ethics.* https://saskschoolboards.ca/wp-content/uploads/2015/08/CodeofEthicsEnglish.pdf

Shapiro, J., & Stefkovich, J. (2022). *Ethical leadership and decision making in education: Applying theoretical perspectives to complex dilemmas* (5th ed.). https://doi.org/10.4324/9781003022862

Sliwka, A. (2010). From homogeneity to diversity in German education. In *Educating Teachers for Diversity: Meeting the Challenge* (pp. 205–217). OECD Publishing. https://doi.org/10.1787/9789264079731-12-en

Statistics Canada. (2022). *Number of students in elementary and secondary schools, by school type and program type.* https://doi.org/10.25318/3710010901-eng

Statistics Finland. (2022a). *Comprehensive schools.* https://stat.fi/en/publication/cl8mo1t49xf0s0dukmzazm0xg

Statistics Finland. (2022b). *Number of comprehensive schools fell further, educational institutions bigger than before.* https://www.stat.fi/til/kjarj/2019/kjarj_2019_2020-02-12_tie_001_en.html

Texas Association of School Boards. (2024a). *Texas school board member code of ethics.* https://www.tasb.org/resources/code-of-ethics

Texas Association of School Boards. (2024b). Leadership TASB (LTASB). https://www.tasb.org/solutions-services/tasb-solutions-services-listing/leadership-tasb

U.S. Department of Education. (2010). *An overview of the U.S. Department of Education.* https://www2.ed.gov/about/overview/focus/what.html#:~:text=The%20U.S.%20Department%20of%20Education%20is%20the%20agency%20of%20the,most%20federal%20assistance%20to%20education

Wallin, D., Young, J., & Levin, B. (2021). *Understanding Canadian schools: An introduction to educational administration* (6th ed.). University of Saskatchewan Open Press. https://openpress.usask.ca/understandingcanadianschools/

York Region District School Board. (2024). *Multi-year strategic plan.* https://www2.yrdsb.ca/board-plans/multi-year-strategic-plan

Zwaagstra, M., Emes, J., Ryan, E., & Palacios, M. (2023). *Where our students are educated: Measuring student enrolment in Canada, 2022.* https://www.fraserinstitute.org/sites/default/files/where-our-students-are-educated-2022.pdf

CHAPTER 4

The Role of Directors and Superintendents: "Lead Learner or CYA/Teflon?"

Abstract In this chapter we consider the role of directors and superintendents in creating, modeling, supporting, and monitoring ethical leadership and healthy workplace cultures in school systems in Canada, the United States, Finland, and Germany. We also provide a vignette of an ethical leadership dilemma of an American assistant superintendent, as well as questions for reader reflection.

Keywords Ethical director/superintendent leadership • Director/superintendent licensure/certification • Director/superintendent ethical leadership standards • Director/superintendent professional organizations

> *"Leadership and learning* are indispensable to each other."
> —John F. Kennedy, former US President

In this chapter we consider the role of directors and superintendents in creating, modeling, supporting, and monitoring ethical leadership and healthy workplace cultures in school systems in Canada, the United States, Finland, and Germany. We also provide a vignette of an ethical leadership dilemma of an American assistant superintendent, as well as questions for reader reflection. As we mentioned at the beginning of Chap. 3 regarding school board members and their boards, in our early experience as school-based leaders, we often felt that the way senior leaders in our district and province operated was "just the way things happened" in all schools and school districts. We learned that we were wrong, and it is our hope that leaders who have only worked in a Canadian or American school district might consider what they might learn from district leaders and governance systems in other parts of our world. If nothing else, this is a provocation to ask more thoughtful, nuanced questions about the ethical leadership of senior leaders in your own context. This chapter provides a glimpse into the work of district or system leaders in Canada, the United States, Germany, and Finland—we know that it is not an exhaustive account.

Ethical Leadership Standards for Directors and Superintendents in Canada

The ethical leadership standards for directors and superintendents in Canada are guided by a number of frameworks and standards across the different provinces and territories. These standards generally emphasize the importance of ethical conduct, integrity, and the establishment of a positive and productive learning environment.

In order to consider these standards for Canadian school superintendents, it is important to have an understanding of the contexts that these district leaders work in. As previously mentioned, there are several different types of school boards in Canada, the main types differentiated by religion and language: public, separate (Roman Catholic or Protestant), or language (Francophone or Anglophone). Canada has a long history of amalgamation or "consolidation" of small local rural districts into larger, more centralized districts—and transporting students long distances (Wallin et al., 2021). For example, in 1946, the British Columbia Ministry of Education rearranged the province's 650 school districts into 74. There were approximately 800 school boards in Canada in the early 1990s (Hickcox, 2022); but, as a result of continuing amalgamation of very small districts into larger districts, in 2021 there were approximately 425 school authorities in the 10 provinces and 3 territories, with 92 of those in the far northern territories (Wallin et al., 2021).

Although always complex, the work of Canadian directors and superintendents can be quite different based on size and location of the district they are leading. For example, the Toronto District School Board (TDSB) is the largest and one of the most diverse school boards in Canada serving approximately 235,000 students throughout the greater Toronto area. So, what does ethical leadership look like for the Director of TDSB who works with a school board of 22 trustees and 600 schools in metro Toronto versus the Executive Director of the Iqaluit District Education Authority (DEA) with a board of seven members (including an Indigenous Elder and a student member) and five schools in the capital city of Nunavut territory?

And from the Provinces: Two Examples

Ontario. In Ontario, the term "supervisory officer" is used to describe directors and superintendents who are school system leaders responsible for student learning, curriculum, pedagogy, teacher and principal development, assessment and evaluation, policy, and legislation—as well as community engagement. Most academic supervisory officers in Ontario come to the role following extensive successful experience as a school principal along with a depth and breadth of system-level curriculum and pedagogical leadership experience (Smith & Qua-Hiansen, 2015). The Ontario College of Teachers (OCT), the self-regulating body for the teaching profession in Ontario, is responsible for establishing and enforcing professional standards and ethical standards applicable to members of the College, for providing for the ongoing education of members of the College, and for accrediting additional qualification (AQ) courses and programs (Ontario College of Teachers, 2023). Teachers who have teaching qualifications in three or more teaching divisions (including the intermediate division), at least five years of successful classroom teaching experience, a master's degree, and a principal's qualification are eligible for the Supervisory Officer's Qualification Program (SOQP).

This credentialing program is built on standards for Ontario teachers and includes separate Standards of Practice and Ethical Standards. It represents the highest level of certification that an educator can achieve with respect to additional teaching qualifications (Smith & Qua-Hiansen, 2015). The Ethical Standards for supervisory officers are focused on care, respect, trust, and integrity. Also fundamental to the standards are an anti-oppression foundation which also identifies leadership ethics:

> It recognizes that educator and student learning and well-being are impacted by biases and assumptions related to power and privilege. Educators have a shared ethical and professional responsibility to identify and challenge indi-

vidual and systemic barriers to support the learning, well-being and inclusion of each learner. (Ontario College of Teachers, 2023, p. 5)

The SOQP is "designed for educational leaders to proactively explore dimensions associated with the effective management of a publicly funded education system by increasing their leadership capacity to effect system and school improvement" (p. 3). This accreditation program consists of four instructional modules, each consisting of at least 50 hours of instruction, and one module consisting of at least 50 hours of practical experience in the workplace. The topics for the instructional modules include Supervisory Officer as System Leader, Governance, Leading System Change, and Accountability—with equity and human rights content compulsory for each module (pp. 10–13). SOQP candidates will identify a Leadership Practicum initiative based on their self-assessment throughout the four modules and in consultation with their SOQP provider and a mentor who is typically a qualified and experienced supervisory officer from the district school board. This practicum involves collaboration with school board staff, school councils, community representatives, employee organizations, and unions or federations. The SOQP requirements must be completed within a five-year period according to the Ontario College of Teachers Act (1996) Reg. 176/10; and, upon successful completion of the SOQP, candidates receive a Supervisory Officer's Certificate in Ontario (Ontario College of Teachers, 2023.)

In addition to the certification requirements, directors and superintendents in Ontario also have a number of professional associations to support their ongoing leadership development. The Ontario Public Supervisory Officers' Association (OPSOA) is designed to champion public education in Ontario, to support aspiring and current members, and to advance leadership-focused learning (Ontario Public Supervisory Officers' Association, 2022). Closely connected to the OPSOA is the Public Council of Ontario Directors of Education (PCODE) which represents the chief education officers and chief executive officers of the 31 public district school boards in Ontario. PCODE and OPSOA have collaborated to create a combined Strategic Plan (Ontario Public Supervisory Officers' Association, 2022). The OPSOA provides a variety of resources for its members and facilitates the operation of the Supervisory Officer's Qualification Program.

Directors and superintendents in Ontario's Catholic districts have a different professional organization of Catholic Supervisory Officers (OCSOA) dedicated to furthering the interests of Catholic Education and to promoting the professional development and welfare of its members (Ontario Catholic Supervisory Officers' Association, 2024a). The OCSOA operates the Supervisory Officers Qualification Program (SOQP) for the Catholic community under the name of the Catholic Community Delivery Organization (CCDO) as an approved provider of the College of Teachers. The vision for their credentialing program is to prepare candidates who will foster, emulate, and promote the distinctive mission of Ontario Catholic schools. They indicate that program graduates will:

> have expanded knowledge, skills, and attitudes to collaboratively set direction, nurture meaningful relationships, promote the growth and development of others, and ensure the accountability of all stakeholders to meet instructional goals, and develop and manage a faith filled school system. (Ontario Catholic Supervisory Officers' Association, 2024b, para. 2)

This program is very similar in structure to the public school supervisory officers' program, including streams for both academic candidates and business candidates.

There also are Francophone supervisory officer programs in Ontario. The OCT provides a Supervisory Officer's Qualification Program Guideline that includes a framework for leadership for supervisory officers in French-language schools.

Alberta. Similarly in Alberta, superintendents and directors must also have a formal leadership credential. The province has two types of certifications for school leaders—leadership certification and superintendent leadership certification. Teachers hired in principal or acting principal roles must hold the leadership certification. Teachers appointed as superintendent of schools (or acting superintendent) must hold both the leadership certification and superintendent leadership certification (Government of Alberta, 2024a). According to the Superintendent of Schools Regulation, superintendents must also hold a master's degree acceptable to the Minister of Education and have three years of experience in the school system. These leadership certifications align with the Leadership Quality Standard (LQS) and Superintendent Leadership Quality Standard (SLQS) developed by the Alberta government.

The Superintendent Leadership Quality Standard (SLQS), which applies only to the one chief superintendent in the school district, focuses on school district operations and supporting the effective governance of elected school trustees. There is general alignment with the leadership standard for principals, but there is explicit mention of ethical leadership in the SLQS. The overarching statement for the Superintendent Leadership Quality Standard indicates:

> Quality superintendent leadership occurs when the superintendent's ongoing analysis of the context, and the superintendent's decisions about what leadership knowledge and abilities to apply, result in quality school leadership, quality teaching and optimum learning for all students in the school authority. (Alberta Education, 2023, p. 2)

In the SLQS competency of Building Effective Relationships, ethical leadership is explicit:

> A superintendent establishes a welcoming, caring, respectful and safe learning environment by building positive and productive relationships with members of the school community and the local community. Achievement of this competency is demonstrated by indicators such as: …(d) modeling ethical leadership practices, based on integrity and objectivity. (Alberta Education, 2023, p. 3)

The difficulty with this standard is that the SLQS does not apply to any of the other senior leaders at the district level who are also credentialed teachers, for example, deputy chief superintendents, superintendents, assistant superintendents, or education directors. The standard that applies to them is the Leadership Quality Standard (LQS) that was created for school-based principals (Alberta Education, 2023). In the LQS, there is no mention of ethical decision-making or ethical/moral leadership behavior. In the leadership competency of Fostering Effective Relationships there is some reference to behaviors which might be characterized as ethical leadership:

> A leader builds positive working relationships with members of the school community and local community. Achievement of this competency is demonstrated by indicators such as: (a) acting with fairness, respect and integrity; (b) demonstrating empathy and a genuine concern for others; (c) creating a welcoming, caring, respectful and safe learning environment; (f) demonstrating a commitment to the health and well-being of all teachers, staff and students; (g) acting consistently in the best interests of students. (Alberta Education, 2023, p. 3)

However, ethical decision-making and ethical/moral leadership behavior are not mentioned. These two standards are Ministerial Orders and also intended to be used in the evaluation of leaders in Alberta.

Superintendents and directors in Alberta have a professional organization called the College of Alberta School Superintendents (CASS) which has undergone a significant change in role based on the provincial government's desire to control the disciplinary process for both system- and school-based leaders. In addition to superintendents, CASS Regulated membership includes a variety of district-level personnel from school districts across the province—including public, Catholic, Francophone, and charter school authorities; these members typically have exempt employee status in their districts. Associate membership is available to system leader positions that are identified within a Collective Agreement between the school district and the Alberta Teachers' Association (ATA); and affiliate membership is available are system leaders for a First Nations school authority in Alberta, are employees of Alberta Education in a senior supervisory or consultative position, are academic members of a university faculty in Alberta, or are members of superintendents' associations in neighboring provinces (College of Alberta School Superintendents, 2024).

Previously CASS had a code of professional conduct referencing ethical leadership, and one of the powers of the organization was to regulate the professional conduct of its members, similar to Ontario. However, if a member was subject to a hearing and disciplinary action, the action would only impact the superintendent's membership in CASS and not employment in their school district.

With the *CASS Act* being introduced in 2022, the legislation was originally written with the intent of CASS having a legal mandate to regulate the conduct of members and potentially make decisions in this area that could have impact upon a member's ability to be a member of CASS, retain certification, and sustain employment as a system education leader with a school authority. (College of Alberta School Superintendents, 2024, para. 2)

For decades, the government of Alberta has generally been very conservative with several versions of right-wing political parties. These conservative governments have had adversarial relationships with the Alberta Teacher's Association, particularly related to the ATA power to discipline its members, including removing certification which has employment consequences.

In March 2022, the government introduced Bill 15, The Education (Reforming Teacher Profession Discipline) Amendment Act and established a different professional discipline model. Bill 15 amended both the existing Education Act and the Teaching Profession Act, with policy-borrowing to "combine the effectiveness of the commissioner model in British Columbia and some arm's-length features of Saskatchewan's Teacher Regulatory Board such as posting upcoming hearing dates to ensure greater transparency" (Government of Alberta, 2024b, para. 4). This model for professional discipline prescribed that "all teachers and teacher leaders (including superintendents) in Alberta are subject to the same disciplinary system under an arm's-length Commissioner model" (College of Alberta School Superintendents, 2024, para. 3). Subsequently, the CASS Board voted by resolution that effective June 2022, all of their existing administrative procedures related to conduct and competency of its members were rescinded. The new disciplinary model, under the direction of the Alberta Teaching Profession Commissioner, came into force on January 1, 2023; and, the role of CASS primarily shifted to providing a continuing education program for its regulated members to complete the Superintendent Leadership Certification (College of Alberta School Superintendents, 2024). The Alberta education ministry has developed a new code of conduct to supplement their teaching and leadership standards, which outlines expectations that certificated teachers and teacher leaders must follow. It outlines the overarching ethical principles that guide everyone in the profession (Government of Alberta, 2024c). (Previously the ATA and CASS dealt with these ethical conduct complaints through their formal processes.) This is a typical example of increased government regulation in the name of "transparency" and "quality assurance" to parents and the public.

In general, the standards and frameworks for superintendents and directors in Canada emphasize the importance of ethical conduct, integrity, collaboration, and the establishment of a positive and productive learning environment. They also highlight the need for career-long professional learning and the development of effective relationships with various stakeholders in the education system.

Ethical Leadership Standards for Directors and Superintendents in the United States

In order to consider ethical leadership standards for American school superintendents and directors, it is important to have an understanding of the contexts that these district leaders work in. During the 2020–21 school year, there were 13,187 public school districts in the United States (Ballotpedia, 2024), and it would be naïve to think that "a school district is just a school district." There are many types of public school districts:

- Elementary school districts educate students who are at lower grade or age levels.
- Secondary school districts educate students who are at higher grade or age levels. These are also known as high school districts.
- A unified school district is a district that provides both elementary and secondary education services and instruction.
- A consolidated or reorganized school district indicates that it was formed from two or more districts.
- A joint school district denotes that the district includes territory from more than one county. A joint state school district means that the district includes territory from more than one state.
- An intermediate school district is a government agency usually organized at the county or multi-county level that assists local school districts in providing programs and services. These districts operate outside the charter of a local school district. The exact role of these agencies varies by state.
- Independent school districts can take different forms depending on the state. In Texas, independent denotes that the district is separate from any county or municipal-level entity. Similarly, in Kentucky, independent districts are separate from county districts. In Minnesota, independent denotes any school district created since July 1, 1957. (Ballotpedia, 2024)

In 2020–21, the largest public school board in the United States was the New York City Department of Education with 912,994 students, followed by the Los Angeles Unified School District with 460,633 students (Ballotpedia, 2024). For a sense of context, California has 1018 school districts in the whole state—each with a superintendent. In Massachusetts, there are 306 school districts with only 405 high schools in the whole state; so, most school districts in Massachusetts are very small—having only one high school. The smallest American public school district is Bois Blanc Pines School District in Michigan with an enrollment of four students. The average school district in the United States has 5.6 schools compared to the 100 largest school districts, which average 155.6 schools per district. So, consider the similarities and differences in the work of over 13,000 public school superintendents across the United States. Does ethical leadership look and feel the same when you are a superintendent to 1867 schools in New York City versus a superintendent to three schools in Amherst, Massachusetts?

Superintendent, chief education officer, or chief executive officer are all titles given to the head administrator of an American school district. They provide leadership and oversight for the students, public schools, and educational services within their district. Superintendents are most often hired by the district's school board; and, in many states, superintendents also serve as non-voting members on the board. The superintendent is responsible for keeping the board informed of events and developments in the district and for making recommendations about changes to daily district operations (Ballotpedia, 2024).

Certainly, education superintendents and directors in the United States are expected to adhere to high ethical leadership standards. These standards are outlined by various professional organizations and also state education departments. The School Superintendents Association (AASA) is a national organization of public school superintendents across the United States. It was formerly known as American Association of School Administrators, and the organizational mission is to advocate "for equitable access for all students to the highest quality public education and [to] develop and support school system leaders" (School Superintendents Association, 2023, para. 4). It has over 10,000 members and describes itself as serving "as the national voice for public education and district leadership on Capitol Hill" (para. 1). The current Code of Ethics of the AASA is long standing and was adopted in 2007. This code of conduct highlights the importance of exemplary professional conduct because of the visibility of the superintendent within their educational community and their local community—"An educational leader's professional conduct must conform to an ethical code of behavior, and the code must set high standards for all educational leaders. The educational leader provides professional leadership across the district and also across the community" (School Superintendents Association, 2007, para. 1).

The AASA standards articulate the importance of honesty, integrity, personal responsibility, public service, and a student focus for decision-making. And, the expectation is that the superintendent will "subscribe to the statements of standards" (para. 3). For example:

The educational leader:

1. Makes the education and well-being of students the fundamental value of all decision-making.
2. Fulfills all professional duties with honesty and integrity and always acts in a trustworthy and responsible manner.
3. Supports the principle of due process and protects the civil and human rights of all individuals.
4. Implements local, state, and national laws.
5. Advises the school board and implements the board's policies and administrative rules and regulations.
6. Pursues appropriate measures to correct those laws, policies, and regulations that are not consistent with sound educational goals or that are not in the best interest of children.
7. Avoids using his/her position for personal gain through political, social, religious, economic, or other influences.
8. Accepts academic degrees or professional certification only from accredited institutions.
9. Maintains the standards and seeks to improve the effectiveness of the profession through research and continuing professional development.
10. Honors all contracts until fulfillment, release or dissolution mutually agreed upon by all parties.
11. Accepts responsibility and accountability for one's own actions and behaviors.
12. Commits to serving others above self. (School Superintendents Association, 2007, para. 4)

And from the States: Two Examples

The various American states have ethical leadership guidelines for superintendents which are also described as ethical standards, codes of ethics, and codes of conduct. (Typically, what determines a code of conduct is either an implicit understanding or an explicit description of sanctions, often related to the employment contract.) And, there are superintendent evaluation processes and documents which make specific reference to ethical leadership behavior.

Wisconsin. Similar to the national School Superintendents Association, in Wisconsin there is a state Wisconsin Association of School District Administrators (WASDA) to provide support for effective executive leadership practice—"Our support ranges from a very personal level in employment and contract matters, to large scale professional development and networking opportunities, to high level representation in the state policy and regulatory environment" (Wisconsin Association of School District Administrators, 2024, para. 1). WASDA has also created an association designed specifically to support the assistants to their superintendents called WASSA—Wisconsin Association of School Superintendent Assistants (WASSA). WASDA has a Code of Ethics which indicates "High standards of ethical behavior for the Professional School Administrator are essential and are compatible with the school administrator's faith in the power of public education and his/her commitment to leadership in the preservation and strengthening of the public schools" (Wisconsin Association of School District Administrators, n.d.). This document is similar in tone and intent to the AASA Code of Conduct. There is an expectation for upholding the honor and dignity of the profession, maintaining high ethical and moral standards, learning throughout career span, carrying out policies and regulations in good faith, being honest in upholding the public trust, and providing the best possible educational experiences/opportunities to everyone in the district. This code of ethics is designed to support and to enhance the performance of individual members and the organization as a whole—and sanctions are not mentioned.

Massachusetts. The *Superintendent and District Administrator Rubric* from the Massachusetts Department of Elementary and Secondary Education (2019) provides a detailed description of expected leadership practice for the superintendent and other district senior leaders across the state which is quite different from the code of ethics of Wisconsin Superintendent Association (or the National American Superintendent Association). This document (in the form of a rubric) which guides the evaluation process for senior leaders in their district is to be used by both the leader and their supervisor to "(1) develop a consistent, shared understanding of what proficient performance looks like in practice, (2) develop a common terminology and structure to organize evidence, and (3) make informed professional judgments about formative and summative performance ratings on each Standard and overall" (p. ii). Although the rubric is designed specifically for the evaluation of the superintendent, "it can also be used by the superintendent for the evaluation of other district level administrators, such as assistant superintendents, directors of curriculum and instruction, school business administrators, and directors of special education" (p. ii). The rubric provides clarity in expectations for all senior leaders to develop system alignment and coherence, to empower other leaders, and to lead with a commitment to equity.

There are many facets of district-based leadership included in this very comprehensive rubric (Massachusetts Department of Elementary and Secondary Education, 2019). Specifically related to ethical leadership, Standard II focuses on Management and Operations and includes a Law, Ethics, and Policies Indicator II-D which explains that the leader "Understands and complies with state and federal laws and mandates, school committee policies, collective bargaining agreements, and ethical guidelines" (p. 15). Exemplary ethical behavior is evident when the superintendent "Models sound, professional judgment; adheres to district's existing code of ethics; protects administrator, student, family, and staff confidentiality appropriately; and effectively supports all staff to do the same" (p. 15). Several of the other indicators in the rubric are closely aligned with ethical leadership behavior as articulated in the Shapiro and Stefkovich framework (2022). For example, the Cultural Proficiency Indicator IV-B explains that the Massachusetts district leader "Ensures that policies and practices enable staff members and students to interact effectively in a culturally diverse environment in which students' backgrounds, identities, strengths, and challenges are respected" (Massachusetts Department of Elementary and Secondary Education, 2019, p. 21). *Exemplary culturally proficient leadership* is evident when the superintendent:

> Leads stakeholders to develop and implement culturally responsive policies that acknowledge the diverse backgrounds, identities, strengths, and challenges of administrators, students and staff. Empowers administrators with time, resources, and support to build culturally responsive learning environments and collaborates with community members to create a culture that affirms individual differences. Models this practice for others. (p. 21)

This rubric describes superintendent performance as Exemplary, Proficient, Needs Improvement, or Unsatisfactory and provides leadership details of behavior in each category.

Generally in the United States, ethical leadership standards for superintendents and directors emphasize student achievement and well-being, integrity, fairness, inclusivity and cultural proficiency, financial accountability, and adherence to laws and policies.

Ethical Leadership Standards for Directors and Superintendents in Finland

In Finland, the ethical leadership standards for superintendents and directors are deeply rooted in the cultural and social foundations of the country. Interestingly, typically in Canada and the United States, superintendents and directors are not part of a teacher union. In Finland, with a long history of strong trade unions, the Trade Union of Education, known as OAJ, is the only labor market organization that protects the interests of education, training, and research sector professionals, including teachers within early childhood education, comprehensive schools, general upper secondary schools, vocational institutes, and universities (Trade Union of Education OAJ, 2020a). Members in this union must work as an employee in education or training or as an education sector expert or manager. In addition to advocating nationally for policies that benefit educators, OAJ negotiates on the national level with employer groups to create universally binding agreements that spell out everything from minimum salaries to working hours for teachers and the length of the school year. The OAJ is the largest member union in the Finnish Confederation of Unions for Academic Professionals (AKAVA), and it also participates in the development of education policy, teaching, and research (OECD, 2007). It is also worth noting that the OAJ is not linked to any political party and is considered a helpful tool in negotiating policies that are turned into national law in Finland.

In Finland, it is practically impossible to become a superintendent or director without also being a former teacher and principal. In terms of ethical leadership, the OAJ is very clear about the importance of ethical behavior, indicating that "good professional ethics are among a teacher's most important resources" (Trade Union of Education OAJ, 2020b, para. 8). The organization has articulated four core values: dignity, truthfulness, fairness, and responsibility and freedom. Each of the core ethical values is explained:

- *Dignity* means respect for humanity. Teachers must respect every person, regardless of gender, sexual orientation, gender diversity, appearance, age, religion, social standing, origin, opinions, abilities, and achievements.
- *Truthfulness* is one of the core values in teachers' basic task, which involves steering learners in navigating life and their environment. Honesty with oneself and others and mutual respect in all communication is a basic aspect of teachers' work.
- *Fairness* is important both when encountering individual learners and groups but also in the work community. Fairness involves in particular promoting equality and non-discrimination and avoiding favouritism.
- Teachers are entitled to their own *values*, but in their work, teachers' responsibility is tied to their basic task and its standards such as legislation and the curriculum. (Trade Union of Education OAJ, 2020b, para. 3–6)

Ethical principles are further outlined for teachers in relation to their work, to learners, to the work community, to stakeholders, to society, and to plurality—For example, related to Finnish teachers and plurality (what we in Canada or the United States would describe as social justice):

> Teachers need to ensure that all learners have the same rights and obligations as members of society. They make sure that learners and their parents' cultures and world views are respected equally and that no one is discriminated against based on them. (para. 14)

In addition, their *Comenius' Oath* is an ethical guideline, created by the Finnish Ethical Committee for the Teaching Profession, that supports teachers' work and serves as a reminder that ethics are the foundation of the teaching profession (Trade Union of Education OAJ, 2020c). The intent is that this oath can be compared to the Hippocratic Oath for physicians and the Archimedean Oath for engineers. The oath can be taken by any qualified teacher regardless of their education level and is designed to strengthen the professional ethics of teachers. It emphasizes the need for teachers "to act fairly and equally in all situations" (para. 3)—and additionally highlights the expertise of teachers to create solidarity within the profession. In the current Finnish structure, it is possible that a school principal, who must be a qualified teacher, might also have a role as a superintendent or director with the local municipal educational administration. All educators are guided by values and general ethical principles that shape educational leadership practices across the nation.

Superintendents have been part of the Finnish educational system for many years, but their role has changed considerably because of education reforms over the last two decades which both have altered the relationship between the national and municipal governments—and also altered how schools are organized, governed, and led (Risku et al., 2014). "The impact of two economic recessions during the 1990s and 2000s and the changes in the statutory government financial transfer system for education have made it difficult for municipalities to employ adequate numbers of education administrative personnel" (p. 389), who would typically be described as superintendents. Consequently, the number of full-time Finnish municipal superintendents of education has gradually decreased over time.

Historically, the requirement of municipal-level school boards was formalized by the School Board Act of 1945, which also stipulated that municipal school boards had to include a teacher representative (Risku et al., 2014). Those teacher representatives were designated to serve both as the secretary of the board and as the executive manager of the municipal comprehensive education system. "Over time, the teacher representative assumed several essential roles including educator, manager, and democratic statesman, which reflect responsibilities assumed by contemporary superintendents. Thus, the teacher-representative position can be regarded as the predecessor of the superintendent position in Finland" (p. 390).

According to the 1968 Act on the Administration of the Municipal Provision of Education, the main task of superintendents was to assist municipal school boards in the preparation, supervision, and execution of local educational issues. Superintendents all had to meet the requirements for teacher qualifications, completing university-based studies in pedagogy and advanced studies in educational administration, as well as having prior teaching administrative experience. "These qualifications provided a strong foundation for superintendents to be able to address effectively their 16 specified work responsibilities" (p. 391). In the 1970s, municipal education superintendents had to implement the comprehensive education system and merge private grammar schools into basic education schools, while contending with the effects of the population shifts—for example, decreasing enrollments in rural areas and increasing enrollments in urban areas.

Although municipal governments are currently required to comply with several Municipal Act statutes, they have considerable discretion in how to structure, govern, and administer their affairs (Risku et al., 2014). The most important requirement is that municipal governments must have a council that enacts rules, regulations, policies, and procedures to govern how work is accomplished. In addition, "the municipal council must establish several oversight boards of which the executive board, election board, and inspection board are obligatory" (p. 387). One important commonality across Finnish municipalities is having separate boards for education. Because municipalities have considerable discretion, educational administrative structures vary greatly. For example, very small municipalities may comply with minimum legal requirements and have a limited structure whereas larger municipalities may have a complex governance and service delivery structure (Risku et al., 2014). Various municipal educational administrations employ directors of educational departments, directors of educational and cultural services, heads of general education divisions, and education development managers—but, typically only in large municipalities. Although these individuals are typically teachers, directors of educational departments might also be individuals without a teacher qualification because "usually the municipal ordinance requires only a master's degree and familiarity with educational administration" (OECD, 2007, p. 39).

The authority and official status of school leaders vary greatly in Finland because according to legislation municipalities are entitled to make independent decisions on their educational administration (OECD, 2007). In the national legislation, a principal's tasks are described very broadly with a general statement that each school shall have a principal who is responsible for the school's operation. "In many small municipalities, a school principal, besides being the director of the educational department, can also administer tasks of other sectoral directors, such as the director of cultural services, the director of sports services, etc." (p. 18). A study of education superintendents in Finland revealed that in 2008, 4.8% of municipalities did not have any staff in their education office, and 21.9% of the municipalities had one individual in the education office (Risku et al., 2014). In some instances, the person responsible for education was the municipal general director, the director of administration, or an office secretary working part-time as the superintendent. In addition, data indicated that 21.4% of municipal [education] superintendents also served as school principals (p. 389). (Although this may have some financial advantages, as would be expected the Association of Finnish Principals recommends that the roles of the superintendent and the principal should not be combined.)

Although the Finnish Ministry of Education abolished its system of school inspection in 1983, such as there still is in Germany, it accomplishes many of the same goals in other ways. "For example, the 1998 Basic Education Act and the Upper Secondary General Education Act obligate municipalities to conduct a self-evaluation and participate in external evaluations of their operations" (Risku et al., 2014, p. 386). The Finnish National Board of Education, which is responsible for the national evaluation of learning outcomes, has an extensive evaluation program that comprises mainly sample-based evaluations in core subjects. These evaluation data are used by municipalities to guide improvement to both comprehensive and upper secondary education.

Superintendents in Finland today have primary responsibility for leading and managing the delivery of education under new government configurations. As the number of municipalities declines, district geographic size and student enrollments increase, which in turn has increased the intensity and complexity of superintendents' work (Risku et al., 2014). Although most municipalities have retained the office of the superintendent, they have changed the job descriptions, responsibilities, and titles to align with the municipalities' strategic plans. Rather than embracing one model of the education superintendency, municipalities are expected to exercise discretion in how to reconfigure the role to fit the needs of different school district operational environments. Finnish superintendents and directors are also sometimes involved in hiring principals and other school staff. The municipalities are entitled to determine themselves how teachers are selected for schools. "These are the main ways: 1. the selection body, which is a politically nominated committee, 2. school boards, 3. the director of each educational department, and 4. principals" (OECD, 2007, p. 23). Often superintendents are now integral parts of the municipalities' executive management team. "Consequently, budget management has become the single most important role of Finnish superintendents' work" (p. 397).

Finnish municipal councils and executive boards have begun to place a high priority on hiring superintendents who are well educated, have teaching and principal experience, and possess thinking that aligns with their municipal strategies. "In their new roles, superintendents are confronted by complex, fragmented, and difficult work demands, and are expected to sort out contradictions between goals, expectations, needs, and resources" (Risku et al., 2014, p. 398). As the demands on superintendents to serve as managers have increased and municipal staff resources have decreased, a number of their tasks have been redirected to school principals and teachers.

In summary, demographic changes, municipal mergers, decline in the number of schools, and need to align education with emerging market economies have presented Finland with formidable leadership challenges. The ethical leadership expectations for superintendents and education directors in Finland are characterized by a commitment to pedagogical leadership, a focus on creating effective learning organizations, and a high level of academic qualification and professional development. These standards are underpinned by a Finnish enduring belief in education as a societal tool and a willingness to evolve the nature and direction of superintendents' work.

ETHICAL LEADERSHIP STANDARDS FOR DIRECTORS AND SUPERINTENDENTS IN GERMANY

In this chapter, our intention is to consider the ethical leadership of educators who are in positions on the executive leadership team in their school districts or authorities. In Germany, there are no specific ethical leadership standards for school leaders, including educators who might be the supervisors of school principals. Typically in Canada or in the United States, there is one superintendent or director who is the only employee of the board of trustees. In the organizational hierarchy, a system leader who is one level below the executive leadership team would generally be the direct supervisor of school principals. We think that it is important to consider in more detail a system that does not have the typical superintendent and director roles that appear in Canada and the United States (and, also in Finland). When we work with German principals, state authorities, and universities, their bureaucratic structure causes us to ask many questions and to check our assumptions. In Germany, we believe the role most similar to the superintendent and director would be school supervisor.

Unless the Basic Law (*Grundgesetz—R1*) awards legislative powers to the federal level, the Länder have the right to legislate in all education sectors, including schools, higher education, adult education, and continuing education (Kultusminster Konferenz, 2018). Detailed regulations are outlined in the constitutions of each Länder (R13–28) and in the separate laws of the Länder. Because each of the Länder has the constitutional authority for autonomy, it is difficult to draw specific similarities in education administrative roles and leadership approaches across the states. "The form of school supervision authorities varies significantly between the 16 German states, from multi-level hierarchies in larger states to a compact school supervision team directly located in the Ministry of Education in city-states" (Dabisch, 2023, p. 6).

Following the founding of the Federal Republic of Germany in 1949, it soon became clear that there was a basic public need for education to be coordinated and harmonized throughout the country if citizens were to be provided with the opportunity of mobility between the Länder in their professional and private lives (Kultusminster Konferenz, 2018). The Standing Conference of the Ministers of Education and Cultural Affairs of the Länder (*Kultusministerkonferenz—KMK*) was developed to provide the coordination necessary to develop shared characteristics and comparability within the education system. In its analysis of educational quality across various countries, for the past 15 years the OECD has identified the need to strengthen teacher quality in early education, general schooling, and vocational and technical education (Organization for Economic Co-operation and Development, 2020). And, the Standing Conference has made quality development and quality assurance in schools one of its central issues. There has been important cooperation between the Federation and the Länder regarding "the assessment of the performance of educational systems in international comparison and in drafting relevant reports and recommendations are discussed in meetings of the Federal Minister of Education and Research and the ministers and senators of the Länder who are responsible for education" (Kultusminster Konferenz, 2018, p. 44).

In Germany, there are a number of levels of administrative responsibility within the education system. Huber's (2020) chapter on the organization of the state education agencies and their role and function governing schools and quality management provides a general, but helpful, overview of the various levels in this traditional bureaucratic model:

At the federal state level is the *Standing Conference of the Ministers of Education and Cultural Affairs* (or KMK). The roles are:

- Suggest and provide recommendations that in return need to be approved by the parliaments of the states
- Negotiate a consensus regarding nationwide educational policies
- Coordinate developments in education across the states

At the highest state (macro) level is the *Education Ministry*. The roles are:

- Governmental and administrative tasks for the respective state
- Strategic management and coordination of tasks
- Organization and structure of administration
- School supervisory authorities at the macro level

At the highest state level there may be a *State Office for Education/School Quality* (but not in all states). The roles are:

- Support of the Ministry in its strategic and conceptual tasks for the respective state
- Implementation of governmental, administrative, and conceptual decisions at the state level

At the middle state (meso) level, which is the district regional level, are *School Supervisory Authorities*. The roles are:

- Implementation of governmental, administrative, and conceptual decisions at the district level
- Advice, support, and control of schools at regional level

At the low state (meso) level, which is subdistrict local or community level, are *School Supervisory Authorities* (in most of the states only for primary education). The roles are:

- Implementation of governmental, administrative, and conceptual decisions at the local level
- Advice, support, and control of schools at local level

At the organizational (micro) level is *School Leadership*. The role is:

- Self-management of schools (Huber, 2020, p. 171)

In larger states like Baden-Württemberg, Bavaria, and North Rhine-Westphalia, this four-level administrative organization is in place. In the smaller states like Bremen, Hamburg, Berlin, the structures are simpler; in Hamburg, for example, only two levels of administration exist.

To provide additional details, the highest state level, the Ministry of Education, "develops policy guidelines in the fields of education, adopts legal provisions and administrative regulations, cooperates with the authorities at national level, and supervises the work of authorities under their purview and of subordinated bodies, institutions and foundations" (Kultusminster Konferenz, 2018, p. 46). The Ministry of Education has its own departments and sections just like other ministries. Again, reflecting the autonomy of the Länder, the allocation of specific responsibilities to the various organizational units is "partly attributable to local developments and partly to ideas on educational policy" (p. 49). The Länder sphere of responsibility includes the detailed regulation of the school's mission and its teaching and educational objectives, described as "internal school matters." The cities, towns, and municipalities are called "school-maintaining bodies," and generally speaking, they are responsible for "external school matters"—for example, school buildings, the procurement and provision of learning and teaching materials, administrative staff and ongoing administration, and the costs for non-teaching staff. "The school-maintaining body is also, as a rule, responsible for school organization measures such as setting up, changing and shutting down schools" (p. 52).

The supervision of schools is complex and includes *Rechtsaufsicht* (legal supervision), *Fachaufsicht* (academic supervision), and *Dienstaufsicht* (supervision of the staff) (Kultusminster Konferenz, 2018). Although the oversight regulations of the 16 states are similar in their requirements, "the organization of the oversight system differs from state to state" (Huber, 2020, p. 173). *Fachaufsicht* (academic supervision) over teaching and educational work (internal school matters) in all public schools is the responsibility of the school supervisory authorities. Academic supervision over primary schools, and lower-level secondary schools such as *Hauptschulen,* is typically done by the low-level school supervisory authorities, where school supervisors who are experienced teachers, often former principals, engage directly with a group of 10–20 schools (Dabisch, 2023). This process has generally been an inspection process. "They are, on the one hand, the superiors of all school staff and, on the other hand, hierarchically subordinate to the central supervision authority and accountable to the Ministry of Education" (p. 53). The Ministries of Education, and sometimes the middle-level school supervisory authorities, supervise all other types of school "and schools of particular importance" (Kultusminster Konferenz, 2018, p. 52).

The school supervisory authorities are expected to check that schools are keeping to the prescribed curricula and *Prüfungsordnungen* (examination regulations) by visiting the school and observing classrooms (Kultusminster Konferenz, 2018). These inspection visits are carried out once a year by an inspection team, often coming from a quasi-independent institute of the respective state. In all states, inspectors not only observe the relevant areas of school quality and report the results to the ministry of the respective school supervisory authority and the school-maintaining body, but they also discuss problems and possible areas of school development with the principal and the teachers. The inspectorate reports to the ministry so that the ministry is able to identify options for improved quality management in the school system, with the focus of the inspection on the quality of instruction. Schools and teachers are assessed based on a quality framework, which varies according to school type. For example, the quality framework of Lower-Saxony contains 16 quality criteria and approximately 100 sub-criteria which vary according to the school type. "During the inspection itself, the inspectors contextualize the school and they evaluate teaching according to the evaluation criteria of the relevant quality framework. The inspectorate emphasizes that only the quality of instruction of the school as a whole is evaluated" (Huber, 2020, p. 174)—not the quality of individual teacher instruction.

Inspections are carried out in four phases: (1) procuring of information regarding the school and preparation of the inspection team, (2) school inspection, (3) distribution of the report to the various stakeholders (school supervisory authority, school administration, teachers, the staff council, the parent and student council, and the legal body in charge of the maintenance of the school), and (4) if necessary, instructions for the school principal to improve certain areas of schooling (Huber, 2020). "If a school is assessed as 'below standard,' the principal is required to consult with school supervisory authorities. Within one year, the school will be re-inspected" (p. 174).

"All states are similar in that although the inspection is a public process, the results are not published (nor do official pupil achievement tables or 'league tables' exist)" (Huber, 2020, p. 173). Based on the historic autonomy of schools and teachers, this inspection process is limited by the individual pedagogical responsibility of the school and the pedagogical responsibility of the teacher. In several Länder, the school supervisory authorities are now legally required to respect the individual pedagogical responsibility of the schools (Kultusminster Konferenz, 2018).

In all Länder, the *Fachaufsicht* (academic supervision) is supplemented by mandatory external evaluation (*Schulinspektion, Schulvisitation*) which is intended to provide the individual schools with information regarding the quality of education provided by the school (Kultusminster Konferenz, 2018). Based on competencies in the respective subjects, students are assessed against state educational standards regarding the knowledge, abilities, and skills the students are expected to have at a certain stage of their school careers (Huber, 2020).

The school supervisory authorities in the Länder also provide *Dienstaufsicht* (staff supervision) for teachers and principals of public schools (Kultusminster Konferenz, 2018). Staffing issues, management, and the general behavior of the individuals working in the school are subject to *Dienstaufsicht*. In some Länder, supervision of staff has been transferred to the principal.

In addition, the Ministry of Education appoints teachers "as consultants for individual subject areas, whose job is to advise and support schools, teachers and officials of the school supervisory authority" (p. 58).

"PISA 2000 not only revealed the mediocre performance of German pupils, in general, in comparison to other OECD states but also revealed considerable differences in school quality among the German states themselves" (Huber, 2020, p. 170). In response, the KMK has focused on aligning the educational policies of the states according to the key features of successful PISA countries—for example, by setting national education standards for all states, by agreeing on a system of regular national monitoring, and by setting standards for teacher professionalization (Organization for Economic Co-operation and Development, 2020).

The latest changes in the school legislation of the Länder reflect the transition of supervisory systems, moving away from centralized and external assessments toward more cooperative and internal means of quality assurance (Huber, 2020). In return for the higher degree of administrative and academic self-responsibility granted to schools, schools in turn must set up school-specific profiles, which articulate the objectives and measures of classroom and school development. This approach to self-evaluation demands a change of the role and duties of the school supervisory authorities:

external checkups are replaced by internal self-evaluations and by external evaluations (such as meta-evaluations of the school self-evaluation reports) as well as by inspections...The task of the school supervisory authorities in the future will increasingly be to assist schools in the interpretation of the results of tests, evaluations, and inspections on school quality, as well as to advise and support schools in their efforts towards school and classroom improvement. (pp. 174–175)

For a number of years, there has been discussion regarding "managerial professionalization for school supervisors along the lines of US superintendents" (Dabisch, 2023, p. 53). With no national leadership standards for educators and professional development not a federal requirement, only a few German states have implemented more standardized professional training for school supervisors (Organization for Economic Co-operation and Development, 2020). As a result, the practice of school supervision is still very dependent on individual school supervisors' experiences and "their perception of the profession with its inherent tensions between pedagogical, advisory, administrative, supportive, and managerial roles" (Dabisch, 2023, p. 54). Although a large portion of the school supervisor's work is focused on the data-based governance model for quality assurance of the particular Länder, supervisors are able to organize a variety of non-data-focused meetings and interactions "and in some cases also educational trips, coffee meetings or even one-to-one coaching sessions for a struggling principal" (p. 60).

There is considerable tension between innovative school leaders and the school supervisory authorities which are more oriented in status quo (Huber, 2020):

> However, education authorities could have a greater impact on quality management of schools...Mainly it is about a differentiated approach to schools. Innovative and high-quality schools need acknowledgement, but schools in challenging circumstances need support and even failing schools need quick and intensive support. (p. 185)

However, as is also typical in Canadian and American systems, the school supervisory authority personnel indicate that they are still tasked with more administrative work than with actual support for schools—and that they are responsible for too many schools to be effective in their support.

Generally while there are neither typical superintendent and director roles nor specific ethical leadership standards for school supervisors in

Germany, we know from our work with schools, school supervisory authorities, and universities that the principles of ethical leadership are recognized and valued at all levels of their education system.

An American Assistant Superintendent's Ethical Dilemma

Karissa had been both a school principal and a district leader in the large school district for over 15 years, so she had a good understanding of the politics of the school board and its relationship with the community. When the new superintendent was hired by the board, the expectation was that the superintendent, who was an experienced senior leader from another state and a member of a racialized community, would assist the district to become more inclusive and innovative related to support for and developing relationships with the racialized students and parents in the district. Karissa, who had enjoyed her work as a district leader, had a reputation for her positive work related to improving teaching practices and learning environments for marginalized students, particularly in her role hiring, supervising, and mentoring school principals. Shortly after the new superintendent arrived, he began to encourage Karissa to apply for a newly created position as assistant superintendent, which was being created by a reorganization of the senior leadership in the school district—to make it similar in structure to the superintendent's previous school district. In this new leadership structure Karissa's previous role changed significantly, so she decided to apply for the position—and became an assistant superintendent.

After working on the executive team with the new superintendent for several months, one of the other newly hired assistant superintendents commented to Karissa that the new superintendent was very political and "Teflon" (e.g., "nothing sticks to them"). Their perspective was that the new superintendent was using this role as a stepping stone to a position in the state education department. The superintendent's message was that to build a strong executive team it was important to have honest, robust conversations, to challenge each other's thinking, and to collaborate to find a solution—and then to speak with one voice to the individual board members or the board as a whole. What Karissa observed was that the superintendent often spoke individually with other executive team members, typically the male finance and human resources leads, and made decisions without consulting the other executive team members. The superintendent then expected the whole team to support those decisions in public.

It became typical that the executive team would spend a full morning preparing for how to deal with the board during upcoming public and private meetings. The superintendent expected to have associate superintendents (or their direct reports) script the superintendent's comments for him to provide the board, as well as their own comments to the board. Karissa began to feel uncomfortable with the way a number of district issues were presented to the board and "spun" to keep board members placated. Karissa spoke candidly in executive team meetings about the complex issues that were facing principals and teachers in schools and cautioned the superintendent related to contentious issues that Karissa knew would create significant negative public reaction for the superintendent, the executive team, and the board—for example, program changes in schools or school closures. Generally, Karissa felt her views were "given airtime" but not actually listened to or understood by the superintendent whose frame of reference for problems continued to be the previous school district and state department where he had worked. Karissa also began to question the breadth of understanding of the superintendent for someone in such an influential role in a very diverse city. For example, during discussions about supporting racialized students, the superintendent was very focused on Black and Indigenous students and seemed puzzled when Karissa indicated that the district also needed to consider the large number of Muslim families from the Middle East and particularly support the many Asian students and families who were currently being targeted because of "prevalent right-wing rhetoric" related to the COVID-19 virus and China.

The superintendent had also indicated that he wanted to have regular "one-on-one touch-base meetings" with each of the executive team members. Frequently these meetings were canceled or rescheduled because of emergent issues that took the superintendent's attention. (Executive team meetings, particularly during the early stages of the COVID-19 pandemic, went overtime for hours with assistant superintendents texting each other privately criticizing how the superintendent was responding to the various challenges—and Karissa wanted to "stay away from" that kind of leadership behavior.) When able to meet individually with the superintendent, Karissa openly shared issues and concerns related to her portfolio, as well as concerns related to communication processes and decision-making in the executive team. Karissa felt the superintendent appeared annoyed with those types of frank discussions and just wanted affirmation of his work.

Quite often the superintendent indicated to the executive team that, even though he was new to the district, he had already developed a network of individual employees at all levels throughout the school district (as well as students) that he relied on for "on the street intel." That approach made Karissa uncomfortable because "it felt underhanded" and certainly not the transparent communication processes that the board had publicly promised parents. And, Karissa worried about the actual impact on the employees and students involved, thinking that they had a friendship and "direct line" to the district superintendent. Karissa had loved her work as a principal in several schools and as a district leader in a number of roles, but this role felt uncomfortable—certainly not work that she enjoyed. After working as an assistant superintendent with the new superintendent for just over a year, Karissa applied for and accepted a senior leader role in another nearby school district.

The chair of the board was very surprised when it was announced that Karissa was leaving the district. Karissa had previously worked with the chair as a board member for the schools in Karissa's section of the city, and they had developed a positive relationship. The chair called Karissa to ask if she would be willing to have a follow-up conversation. (Neither the superintendent nor anyone from their human resources department had asked Karissa to participate in an exit interview or had any other conversation about her leaving the district. However, the superintendent was effusive about Karissa's excellent work and his "best wishes" in scripted communication with the system leaders, school-based leaders, and the board.) In their conversation, the chair asked why Karissa had decided to leave. Karissa responded that although she had loved her work in the district she could not continue to work with the superintendent because of the "scripted and sanitized" conversation with the board, knowing the position board members would be put in with their communities. Karissa also indicated that quite often questions that board members had asked the superintendent were not answered truthfully, in Karissa's opinion—which had been shared with the superintendent, but which the superintendent had ignored. Karissa said there were decisions made by the executive team that Karissa did not want her reputation as an educator associated with. The chair did not ask for specific examples; and, Karissa didn't volunteer further detail. In a very professional response, the chair was apologetic that Karissa was not happy in the new role and sorry to see her leave. In the brief meeting, the final comment from the chair was to thank Karissa for her candid comments and to indicate that it would help them ask the superintendent and executive team "better questions in the future."

The superintendent continued with the district for another two years but did not compete his five-year term or move to a position in the state education department—but instead moved to another superintendent position in a smaller school district in a different state.

Questions to Consider

- Thinking about the Shapiro and Stefkovich multiparadigm framework (2022), how does the ethic of the profession relate to this leadership dilemma?
- How does the ethic of care apply to this situation?
- Considering the typical American standards for superintendents and directors, what might have been the ethical issues related to the behavior/approach of the superintendent?
- Was it ethical for the chair of the board to ask the assistant superintendent to do an exit interview? And, was it ethical for the assistant superintendent to participate?
- Which of the signs of a healthy work culture or toxic work culture were evident in this leadership vignette?

The first responsibility of a leader is to define reality. The last is to say thank you. In between, the leader is a servant.
—Max DePree, former American businessman and writer

REFERENCES

Alberta Education. (2023). *Superintendent leadership quality standard: Ministerial Order #0203/2020 (amended 2023)*. https://open.alberta.ca/publications/superintendent-leadership-quality-standard

Ballotpedia. (2024). *Public school district*. https://ballotpedia.org/Public_school_district_(United_States)

College of Alberta School Superintendents. (2024). *Professional conduct review.* https://cass.ab.ca/about-cass/professional-conduct-review/

Dabisch, V. (2023). The practices of data-based governance: German school supervision, professionalism and datafied structurations. *Tertium Comparationis, 29*(1), 48–72. https://doi.org/10.31244/tc.2023.01.03

Government of Alberta. (2024a). *Leadership certifications.* https://www.alberta.ca/leadership-certifications

Government of Alberta. (2024b). *Reforming teacher profession discipline processes.* https://www.alberta.ca/reforming-teacher-profession-discipline-processes

Government of Alberta (2024c). *Code of professional conduct for teachers and teacher leaders.* https://open.alberta.ca/publications/code-of-professional-conduct-for-teachers-and-teacher-leaders

Hickcox, E. (2022). School boards. *The Canadian Encyclopedia.* https://www.thecanadianencyclopedia.ca/en/article/school-boards

Huber, S. (2020). Germany: Education state agencies in Germany: Their organization, role and function in school governing and quality management. In H. Ärlestig & O. Johansson (Eds.), *Educational authorities and the schools. Educational governance research, vol. 13.* Springer. https://doi.org/10.1007/978-3-030-38759-4_10

Kultusminster Konferenz. (2018). *Education system in the Federal Republic of Germany 2018/19.* https://www.kmk.org/fileadmin/Dateien/pdf/Eurydice/Bildungswesen-engl-pdfs/organisation_and_governance.pdf

Massachusetts Department of Elementary and Secondary Education. (2019). *Massachusetts model system for educator evaluation: Superintendent and district administrator rubric.* https://www.doe.mass.edu/edeval/model/PartIII_AppxA.pdf

Ontario Catholic Supervisory Officers' Association. (2024a). *Who we are.* https://ocsoa.ca/who-we-are/

Ontario Catholic Supervisory Officers' Association. (2024b). *Program & module overview.* https://ocsoa.ca/soqp/program-overview/

Ontario College of Teachers. (2023). *Supervisory officer's qualification program guideline.* https://www.oct.ca/-/media/PDF/Additional%20Qualifications/Supervisory%20Officers/EN/final_program_supervisory_officers_qualification_e.pdf

Ontario Public Supervisory Officers' Association. (2022). *OPSOA/PCODE strategic plan.* https://www.opsoa.org/about/strategic-plan

Organization for Economic Co-operation and Development. (2007). *Improving school leadership—Finland: Country background report.* https://www.oecd.org/education/school/38529249.pdf

Organization for Economic Co-operation and Development. (2020). *Education policy outlook: Germany.* https://www.oecd.org/education/policy-outlook/country-profile-Germany-2020.pdf

Risku, M., Kanervio, P., & Björk, L. (2014). Finnish superintendents: Leading in a changing education policy context. *Leadership and Policy in Schools, 13*(4), 383–406. https://doi.org/10.1080/15700763.2014.945653

Shapiro, J., & Stefkovich, J. (2022). *Ethical leadership and decision making in education: Applying theoretical perspectives to complex dilemmas* (5th ed.). https://doi.org/10.4324/9781003022862

Smith, D., & Qua-Hiansen, J. (2015). Democratic dialogue as a process to inform public policy: Reconceptualizing a supervisory officer's qualification program. *International Journal of Educational Policy & Leadership, 10*(1), 1–32. https://files.eric.ed.gov/fulltext/EJ1138619.pdf

The School Superintendents Association. (2007). *Code of ethics.* https://www.aasa.org/about-aasa/Code-of-Ethics

The School Superintendents Association. (2023). *About AASA.* https://www.aasa.org/about-aasa

Trade Union of Education OAJ. (2020a). *Education sector policy.* https://www.oaj.fi/en/policies/

Trade Union of Education OAJ. (2020b). *Teacher's values and ethical principles.* https://www.oaj.fi/en/education/ethical-principles-of-teaching/teachers-values-and-ethical-principles/

Trade Union of Education OAJ. (2020c). *Comenius' oath for teachers.* https://www.oaj.fi/en/education/ethical-principles-of-teaching/comenius-oath-for-teachers/

Wallin, D., Young, J., & Levin, B. (2021). *Understanding Canadian schools: An introduction to educational administration* (6th ed.). University of Saskatchewan Open Press. https://openpress.usask.ca/understandingcanadianschools/

Wisconsin Association of School District Administrators. (2024). *Wisconsin Association of School District Administrators.* https://www.wasda.org/

Wisconsin Association of School District Administrators. (n.d.) *Code of ethics.* https://cdn.ymaws.com/www.wasda.org/resource/resmgr/About_WASDA/wasdacode.pdf

CHAPTER 5

The Work of School Principals: "Where the Buck Stops!"

Abstract In this chapter, we examine the work of the school principal considering the influence of the societal and cultural context in which their schools and school systems are located. Similarities regarding the ethical leadership expectations for school principals across Canada, the United States, Germany, and Finland will be described—as well as differences. Consideration will be given to the licensure standards for school principals that require an understanding of ethical issues and the expectation for ethical leadership behavior. We also provide reflections on ethical leadership from principals in the four countries and questions for reflection.

Keywords Ethical school principal leadership • Principal certification/licensure • Principal ethical leadership standards • Principal professional organizations

> "A leader takes people where they want to go. A great leader takes people where they don't necessarily want to go, but ought to be."
> —Rosalynn Carter, former US First Lady

In this chapter, we examine the work of the school principal considering the influence of the societal and cultural context in which their schools and school systems are located. Similarities regarding the ethical leadership expectations for school principals across Canada, the United States,

© The Author(s), under exclusive license to Springer Nature Switzerland AG 2024
B. Yee, D. Yee, *International Perspectives on Ethical Educational Leadership*, https://doi.org/10.1007/978-3-031-70839-8_5

Germany, and Finland will be described—as well as differences. Consideration will be given to the licensure standards for school principals that require an understanding of ethical issues and the expectation for ethical leadership behavior. We also provide reflections on ethical leadership from principals in the four countries and questions for reflection. As we have explained at the beginnings of Chaps. 3 and 4, in our early experience as school-based leaders, we often felt that the way our district and province operated was "just the way things happened" in all schools and school districts. We learned that we were wrong, and it is our hope that leaders who have only worked in a Canadian or American school district might consider what they might learn from school principals in other parts of our world. If nothing else, this is a provocation to ask more thoughtful, nuanced questions about ethical principal leadership in our own contexts. This chapter provides a glimpse into the work of principals in Canada, the United States, Germany, and Finland—again, we know that it is not an exhaustive account.

Policies and behaviors in school districts are certainly impacted by their national and regional contexts. Standards for ethical educational leadership are being discussed and implemented in various ways in a variety of countries; however, the connection between ethical school-based leadership and a healthy or toxic workplace culture in schools is rarely researched or discussed. As you read about the work of school principals in this chapter, please consider what further questions need to be asked about a principal's influence on school culture.

ETHICAL LEADERSHIP STANDARDS FOR PRINCIPALS IN CANADA

In Canada, principal leadership standards for principals vary by province, although they articulate similar themes related to a commitment to students, their learning, and well-being, to instructional leadership, and to ongoing professional learning. However, there are important differences related to ethical leadership. One of the complexities of principal leadership in Canada is their contractual relationship to the teaching staff of their schools, which differs province by province. In Alberta, principals and assistant principals are part of the same bargaining unit as teachers, the Alberta Teachers' Association (ATA). In both Ontario and British

Columbia, principals and vice-principals are not part of the teacher unions, the Ontario Teachers' Federation (OTF) and the BC Teachers' Federation (BCTF).

The Province of Ontario

In Ontario, the Ontario College of Teachers (OCT), which was created by the Ontario College of Teachers Act in 1996, regulates the teaching profession in the interest of the Ontario public. Its role is to set standards for the profession (including ethical standards) and to issue, suspend, or revoke teaching certificates. The OCT has developed Ethical Standards for the Teaching Profession focusing on care, respect, trust, and integrity (Ontario College of Teachers, 2024). On the other hand, the Ontario Teachers' Federation (OTF) is essentially a teachers' union responsible for advocating on behalf of the profession. There are four affiliates of the Ontario Teachers' Federation (OTF): the Association des enseignantes et des enseignants franco-ontariens (AEFO); the Elementary Teachers' Federation of Ontario (ETFO); the Ontario English Catholic Teachers' Association (OECTA); and the Ontario Secondary School Teachers' Federation (OSSTF). All teachers in Ontario's publicly funded schools belong to one of these affiliates and to OTF. School principals and vice-principals are not part of the OTF or an affiliate. However, principals and vice-principals are members of OCT and are subject to the same professional standards, including their ethical standards. They are voluntarily represented by the Ontario Principals' Council, Catholic Principals' Council of Ontario, and l'Association des directions et directions adjointes des écoles francoontariennes.

The Ontario Leadership Framework (OLF), which applies to principals and vice-principals, was first introduced in 2006 and revised in 2013. The OLF is not a Ministerial Order, but was developed by the Institute for Educational Leadership (IEL) which brings together representatives from many of Ontario's educational leadership organizations—principal's associations, supervisory officers' associations, councils of directors of education, the Ontario Association of Senior Business Officials, and the Ministry of Education—to work in a collaborative partnership and model effective leadership at all levels in the province. The mission of the IEL is to "influence educational leadership policy/practices in Ontario, support the development of educational leaders, and contribute to research on educational leadership in Ontario and globally" (Ontario Institute for Educational Leadership, 2024a, para. 2). The 2022–26 strategic plan is labeled "Supporting Ethical Leadership in Ontario"—bringing focus to ethical leadership in the province. The OLF itself outlines five core leadership capacities, "1) Setting goals; 2) Aligning resources with priorities; 3) Promoting collaborative learning cultures; 4) Using data; and 5) Engaging in courageous conversations" (Ontario Institute for Educational Leadership, 2013, p. 8). There are a number of very detailed and prescriptive frameworks specific to public and Catholic schools within the OLF; for example, School-level Leadership, Catholic School-level Leadership, System-level Leadership, Catholic System-level Leadership, K-12 School Effectiveness Framework, and District Effectiveness Framework. However, there is no specific description of or framework for ethical leadership other than a comment related to online OLF "leadership stories." "The purpose of the stories is to promote dialogue and discussion of the leadership practices and PLRs as a way of reflecting on and strengthening your own practice as an ethical leader" (Ontario Institute for Educational Leadership, 2024b, para. 1). There appears to be an assumption that if there is a positive and inclusive educational environment for students and staff in a school that there is also ethical leadership.

There has been recent criticism that this OLF framework was created primarily from traditional, white male-oriented leadership perspectives nearly ten years ago and needs to be updated to be more relevant to specific "equity-seeking groups (e.g., women, Indigenous, Black, Brown, LGBTQ2S+ or those living with a disability)" (Doan & Jaber, 2021, p. 2). Also, some Ontario school districts have determined the importance of being more specific regarding ethical leadership. York Region School District Board (YRDSB) (2020), for example, developed a leadership framework that complements the OLF, with a focus on making ethical leadership competencies clear. This framework includes actions for leaders that emphasize ethical practices, such as engaging in critical self-reflection to examine their leadership and developing a shared understanding of ethical leadership. Their district strategic actions included: create a working definition of ethical leadership (EL); build ethical leadership competency and consciousness in all aspects of school and department leaders' work (e.g., decision-making, relationship building, problem-solving, communicating, monitoring of impact); and, strengthen the focus on ethical leadership in the [district] leadership strategy. In their definition of ethical leadership practice, they reference the work of the B.C. Principals' and Vice-Principals' Association.

The Province of British Columbia

In British Columbia, the BC Teachers' Federation (BCTF) has a Code of Ethics which provides general rules for teachers in maintaining high standards of professional service and ethical conduct toward students, colleagues, and the professional union. However similar to Ontario, principals and vice-principals are not part of the British Columbia Teachers' Federation; they are represented by the B.C. Principals' and Vice-Principals' Association (BCPVPA) which is a voluntary professional association representing school leaders employed in B.C.'s public education system.

The Leadership Standards for Principals and Vice-Principals in British Columbia (BCPVPA, 2019) were first established in 2007 and were updated in 2020. Compared to the Alberta principal leadership standards which are a Ministerial Order intended to guide evaluation processes, the British Columbia leadership standards were developed by the B.C. Principals' and Vice-Principals' Association (BCPVPA):

> to foster continuous professional learning and development in working towards effective leadership. The Leadership Standards, as they are written, are generic, context dependent and aspirational. As such, this document may be used to help frame individual professional growth plans that support sustainability and best practice; it is not intended as an instrument for evaluation or judgment of the individual performance of Principals and Vice-Principals. (2019, p. 3)

In this standard, there are four leadership domains: Ethical Leadership, Instructional Leadership, Relational Leadership, and Organizational Leadership. Ethical leadership is very prominent in this framework, "The Ethical Leadership domain focuses on the Principals' and Vice-Principals' role in setting and sustaining a sense of moral purpose and in making ethical decisions within schools" (p. 11). In the Ethical Leadership domain there are two standards. Standard 1: Leading a Community of Caring and Learning—"Principals and Vice-Principals guide the development and implementation of shared values, vision, mission, and goals to support engagement, learning, and success for all learners." And, Standard 2: Decision-making—"Principals and Vice-Principals articulate a process of decision-making using an ethical framework based on the moral purpose and direction of the school." In each of these standards, there are action statements for leaders as well as reflective questions, for example, in

Standard 2—"Model ethical practice and decision-making based on shared core values and beliefs. Develop and implement protocols and processes based on a strong ethical framework…Understand the requirements of the BCPVPA Code of Ethics, Code of Professional Practice, School Act and TRB Standards" (p. 13). One of the important additions in the most recent update is the inclusion of British Columbia First Peoples Principles of Learning related to each of the leadership standards. For Standard 2, "Learning involves recognizing the consequences of one's actions. Learning recognizes the role of Indigenous knowledge" (p. 13).

The Province of Alberta

In Alberta, the Leadership Quality Standard (LQS) is a Ministerial Order which applies to school-based principals, assistant/vice-principals and system leaders. In the Leadership Quality Standard (LQS) for principals, ethical leadership is not explicitly articulated or an expected behavior. The overarching statement for the Leadership Quality Standard indicates a focus on "optimum learning" for all students: "Quality leadership occurs when the leader's ongoing analysis of the context, and decisions about what leadership knowledge and abilities to apply, result in quality teaching and optimum learning for all school students" (Alberta Education, 2023a, p. 2). In the leadership competency of Fostering Effective Relationships there is reference to behaviors which might be characterized as ethical leadership in several of the indicators:

> 1. A leader builds positive working relationships with members of the school community and local community. Achievement of this competency is demonstrated by indicators such as: (a) acting with fairness, respect and integrity; (b) demonstrating empathy and a genuine concern for others; (c) creating a welcoming, caring, respectful and safe learning environment; (f) demonstrating a commitment to the health and well-being of all teachers, staff and students; (g) acting consistently in the best interests of students. (Alberta Education, 2023a, p. 3)

However, ethical decision-making and ethical/moral leadership behavior are not mentioned.

As mentioned in Chap. 4, the Alberta Superintendent Leadership Quality Standard (SLQS), which applies only to the one head superintendent in the district, is aligned with the standard for principals and focuses on school district operations and supporting the effective governance of elected school trustees. However, there is explicit mention of ethical leadership in the SLQS. In the SLQS competency of Building Effective Relationships ethical leadership is explicit:

> 1. A superintendent establishes a welcoming, caring, respectful and safe learning environment by building positive and productive relationships with members of the school community and the local community. Achievement of this competency is demonstrated by indicators such as: ...(d) modeling ethical leadership practices, based on integrity and objectivity. (Alberta Education, 2023b, p. 3)

This inconsistency in the leadership standards presents mixed messages for educational leaders across Alberta school districts. And, the application of these standards varies widely across the 62 school districts in the province.

The Alberta Teachers' Association (ATA) also had a Code of Professional Conduct which was used as a standard in cases of complaints related to teacher and principal behavior. (In Alberta, school principals were typically members of the ATA and also bound by their code of conduct; only district leaders who became "exempt" employees of the school district were not part of the association.) Recently, the authority of the ATA in Alberta has changed significantly. In May 2022, the government passed Bill 15, The Education (Reforming Teacher Professional Discipline) Amendment Act, requiring a new code of conduct to be in place on January 1, 2023. This is the same date that the Alberta Teaching Profession Commission, which is now responsible for investigating allegations that a teacher has broken the code of conduct, came into effect. Several parts of the previous code have been carried forward, with the province's conservative government including a narrative that the new code provides a more impartial process and more safety for students and parents (Government of Alberta, 2024).

In Canada, school principals have expectations for ethical leadership behavior, whether through frameworks created through their certification bodies and/or their professional associations—some very explicit and some not as well understood. The examples from the three provinces illustrate some of the differences between the provinces based on the principal's contractual relationship to the teaching staff of their schools, which differs province by province. There are no national standards for school principal ethical leadership.

Ethical Leadership Standards for Principals in the United States

In the United States, The National Policy Board for School Administration (NPBSA), updated its Professional Standards for Educational Leaders (PSEL) in 2015. These standards apply to principals and assistant principals, and they also apply to school district leaders. Developing the standards with a variety of national principal, school board, and university associations, the standards:

> define the nature and the quality of work of persons who practice that profession, in this case educational leaders. They are created for and by the profession to guide professional practice and how practitioners are prepared, hired, developed, supervised, and evaluated. They inform government policies and regulations that oversee the profession. (NPBSA, 2015, p. 2)

These updated standards reflect the complexity of educational leadership in current contexts, including ethics and professional norms, and they advance areas of principal work that were once not well understood or deemed less relevant but more recently have been shown to contribute to student learning:

> It is not enough to have the right curriculum and teachers teaching it, although both are crucial. For learning to happen, educational leaders must pursue all realms of their work with an unwavering attention to students…The Standards recognize the central importance of human relationships not only in leadership work but in teaching and student learning. (p. 3)

These standards inform the National Educational Leadership Preparation Standards (NELP) and the Accreditation Review Process. They also guide the preparation of aspiring educational leaders and the process by which state and university preparation programs seek accreditation from the Council for the Accreditation for Educational Preparation (CAEP). Specific to Standard 2—Ethics and Professional Norms, the standard clearly outlines expectations for the ethical behavior of principals to foster student academic success and well-being:

(a) Act ethically and professionally in personal conduct, relationships with others, decision-making, stewardship of the school's resources, and all aspects of school leadership.
(b) Act according to and promote the professional norms of integrity, fairness, transparency, trust, collaboration, perseverance, learning, and continuous improvement.
(c) Place children at the center of education and accept responsibility for each student's academic success and well-being.
(d) Safeguard and promote the values of democracy, individual freedom and responsibility, equity, social justice, community, and diversity.
(e) Lead with interpersonal and communication skill, social-emotional insight, and understanding of all students' and staff members' backgrounds and cultures.
(f) Provide moral direction for the school and promote ethical and professional behavior among faculty and staff. (p. 10)

The standards describe "a positive approach to leadership that is optimistic, emphasizes development and strengths, and focuses on human potential" (p. 3). The PSELs are not the only set of standards for educational leaders in the United States. Each state generally has its own set of standards that align with the PSELs or may have additional requirements.

The State of California

As an example, the California Professional Standards for Education Leaders (CPSEL) were initially developed in 2001 and outline what an effective leader in the context of California schools must know and be able to do. "They are a set of broad policy standards that are the foundation for administrator preparation, induction, development, professional learning and evaluation in California" (California Commission on Teacher Credentialing, 2014, p. 1). While much has changed in the two decades since the advent of the standards and subsequent updates, the key tenets have remained the same, "to reach every student and support every teacher in meeting increasingly complex outcomes demands a cadre of increasingly committed and effective administrators" (p. 3). Foundational competencies for California state instructional leaders are: "(1) Development and implementation of a shared vision; (2) Instructional leadership, management and learning environment; (3) Family and community engagement; (4) Ethics and integrity; and (5) External context and policy" (p. 3). Ethical leadership is explicit in these state standards. The overall descriptor for the Ethics and Integrity competency is "Education leaders make decisions, model, and behave in ways that demonstrate professionalism, ethics, integrity, justice, and equity and hold staff to the same standard" (p. 9). Related to ethical leadership, the CPSEL articulates the elements of reflective practice, ethical decision-making, and ethical action. In each one of these elements, specific actions and examples of how leaders may demonstrate these standards in their daily work are provided. For example, Element 5C: Ethical Action expects that "Leaders recognize and use their professional influence with staff and the community to develop a climate of trust, mutual respect, and honest communication necessary to consistently make fair and equitable decisions on behalf of all students" (p. 9). There are five specific indicators to guide principals regarding the Ethical Action element, for example, "Indicator 5C-2 - Use a variety of strategies to lead others in safely examining personal assumptions and respectfully challenge beliefs that negatively affect improving teaching and learning for all students" (p. 10). These indicators provide clear direction for ethical action, as well as thoughtful questions for principal reflection.

In the United States there are national standards for the ethical leadership of school principals. As illustrated by the California example, typically there are state standards which align with those national standards but are often more specific and tailored to the state context.

ETHICAL LEADERSHIP STANDARDS FOR PRINCIPALS IN GERMANY

Similar to Canada, the country's education system is quite decentralized, with the 16 German Länder (states) primarily responsible for each of their education systems. Teacher and principal certification processes vary depending on the Länder. In Germany, there are no specific national standards for school leaders (Klein & Schwanenberg, 2022). There also are no specific codes of conduct or ethical codes for teachers or school principals. In 2004, the Ministers of Education across the Länder began focusing on developing an agreement on standards for teacher education to support further development of the whole German education system in order to enable all children and young people to achieve educational success and social participation through national guidelines for the training and daily work of teachers (Sekretariat der Kultusministerkonferenz, 2004). Their work on developing national coherence in teaching practice is ongoing.

School leaders in Germany are typically head teachers (referred to as *Rektor*) who take on leadership roles while still teaching with a reduced course load. In all Länder, head teacher candidates must hold the qualifications necessary to teach at that school level or school type and have several years of teaching and management experience. Commitment to in-service teacher training is identified as one factor typically considered in a teacher's application to become a head teacher. Head teacher responsibilities and duties are set out in the Länder Education Acts and in specific regulations for such roles. The head teacher, subject to the legal and administrative regulations of the school supervisory authority, is also authorized to issue instructions to the other members of the teaching staff and the non-teaching personnel within the framework of duties relating to staff supervision (*Dienstaufsicht*) and academic supervision (*Fachaufsicht*) (European Commission, 2023). These duties may include managing staff and the school budget; evaluating teachers; planning school-level professional development; and creating a school development plan with goals aligned to state-level quality frameworks. The Länder ministries of education are typically responsible for hiring school leaders, although in some cases it is done by the local school authority (NCEE, 2017).

The role of principals in Germany has evolved over time. Traditionally, principals were teachers with additional administrative tasks who "kept the school running" but were not responsible for school improvement or the professional learning of their faculty of largely autonomous teachers. To support the principal and deputy principal, organizational and administrative tasks (e.g., planning the school timetable, operating of the school library) may be transferred to individual teachers. In addition, the Ministry of Education and Cultural Affairs in the Länder appoints teachers as consultants for individual subject areas, whose job is to advise and support schools, teachers, and officials of the school supervisory authority. The classroom hours of these teachers are reduced to allow them to carry out their administrative and consultative functions (European Commission, 2023). More recently, with reforms in public administration as well as adoption of concepts from North American school effectiveness research, principals are expected to be "leaders for learning" as well (Klein & Bronnert-Härle, 2020). The principal now typically has a particular responsibility for quality development and for managing change processes in their individual school. They assume this responsibility together with the local school supervision authorities and the support systems and institutions of the Länder (European Commission, 2023).

There is no federally required training or specific qualifications for school principals in Germany (Tulowitzki et al., 2019). Also, there is no unified job description or evaluation framework for leadership competence of German principals. Most of the Länder do, however, provide additional qualification/training for school leaders after they have been hired, although this is often voluntary. In addition to training for new school leaders, some Länder have more recently developed preparatory training for aspiring leaders. For example, since 2009, teachers in Bavaria are required to complete a two-year preparatory course before submitting an application for a "school head" position. This training is organized and paid for by the Länder. Some Länder, but not all, also offer continuing professional development, such as coaching or advice on implementing quality improvement processes (NCEE, 2017). There has been discussion as to the value of creating a standardized federal qualification for principals with questions related to principal leadership professionalism and school autonomy, including localized quality control (Tulowitzki et al., 2019).

In contrast to the United States and Canada, German principals generally receive little support from the local or state authorities when it comes to school improvement, and there are very few networks or other collaborative structures between schools at local level. Many principals in Germany have not received any formal training for their new role (Klein & Schwanenberg, 2022), which is partly because, while the normative and legal expectations of the principal's role have changed, the systemic structures and processes for the recruitment and training of principals are only slowly adapting to the changed role (Tulowitzki et al., 2019). Only recently have Länder begun to develop processes for systematic evaluation, feedback, and support structures for principals (Klein & Schwanenberg, 2022).

The principle of shared staff responsibility for education and a strong history of German teacher autonomy applies in all Länder (European Commission, 2023). The principal usually convenes and chairs the formal group where all teachers from the whole school meet to discuss matters of shared interest (*Lehrerkonferenz*). For example, one of the tasks of the teachers' conference is to select textbooks from the lists of textbooks approved by the Ministry. In addition, the teachers' conference is also responsible for deciding on individual disciplinary measures, up to and including expulsion, in conflict situations (European Commission, 2023). Principals and deputy principals often do not see themselves as leaders of their schools, are often concerned that their leadership will not be accepted by teachers, and feel less confident when it comes to encouraging teachers to be more reflective about their work (Klein and Bronnert-Härle, 2020). A recent study by Hancock et al. (2019) on the motivation of German principals to assume that role highlights the issue that principal leadership development occurs after a teacher accepts their role as principal. The findings indicate that German teachers "may be more motivated to pursue the principalship if they receive training to better prepare themselves for success before being hired as a principal" (p. 95).

In Germany, there are no national or Länder-specific principal leadership standards of practice. We also were unable to uncover specific ethical leadership expectations or codes of conduct for school principals, as the German education system continues to evolve in their approach to of school leadership.

ETHICAL LEADERSHIP STANDARDS FOR PRINCIPALS IN FINLAND

Finland is among those European nations that have moved swiftly from an agrarian society to urbanization and an industrialized culture. This led to a development in which between the 1960s and the 1990s the Finnish education system not only aligned itself with the state, but also increased its role and importance as a route to higher social status and wealth (Jantunen et al., 2022). Schools have a long tradition of promoting national unity. Finnish nationalism arose in the late nineteenth century, and it is not unusual that, at least to some extent, Finnish principals and teachers still maintain these traditional values in schools and teaching—"Topelian patriotism and his [Zachris Topelius] worldview has had a strong influence on the construction of Finnish identity" (p. 2). When the Finnish national compulsory education system was formed in the 1970s, the main objective was developing a strong ethos composed of shared values that strengthened Finland's national identity. However, the Finnish population is becoming more diversified in terms of language and cultural background; this is reflected in both school life and school leadership. The objective in terms of education policy had been to ensure equal opportunities in education for immigrants, with the numbers steadily increasing (Ministry of Education, Finland, 2007). Recently, there has been an increase in Finnish educational research concerning the concept of diversity. Research has moved away from a focus on multiculturalism and toward exploring cultural diversity and identity. Currently, the role of a principal is central in developing a school community that values diversity and experiences it as a richness and an asset (Jantunen et al., 2022).

Teachers and principals in Finland are well respected by their communities, and principals are highly qualified professionals. The qualification requirements for principals are based on their experience as teachers and their studies in educational administration (Lahtero et al., 2019). Principals must hold a five-year master's degree, a teacher qualification, work experience as a teacher, and excellent knowledge of the school's official language (either Finnish or Swedish.) Additionally, they must have a certificate in educational administration or have completed university-level studies in educational leadership and administration. However, there is no unified job description or evaluation framework for leadership competence of Finnish principals. "Trust is laid upon high-standard teacher education, principal training and continuing professional education taking place in the world of work" (Ministry of Education, Finland, 2007, p. 25). Principals have among the highest degree of autonomy compared to their European peers. They also have the most permanent employment status among teaching staff—typically, a principal's position comes with lifetime tenure, a common practice in Finland. Although more recently, some local municipal authorities may appoint principals for six- or seven-year terms (National Center on Education and the Economy, 2023).

Both Finnish teachers and principals value professional learning throughout their careers. The leadership training for principals is divided into five different categories:

- Principal preparation or qualification programs
- Specialist qualification programs
- In-service training programs
- Continuing professional development programs and
- School-based professional development programs

These programs generally address issues such as management of human and financial resources, school laws, curriculum development and planning, problem-solving and decision-making skills, ethical reasoning, school-family partnerships, learning and program evaluations, and information and communication technologies (Kakon et al., 2014). During leadership training in Finland, practical field work sessions are also organized, providing prospective principals with the day-to-day leadership expectations and realities in Finnish schools (National Center on Education and the Economy, 2023).

As mentioned in Chaps. 3 and 4, due to the decentralized nature of the Finnish system and the autonomy of their municipal educational authorities, the range of responsibilities and duties assigned to schools and principals varies (Jantunen et al., 2022). In national legislation, a principal's tasks are described very broadly with a general statement that each school must have a principal who is responsible for the school's operation. Additionally, by means of decrees, responsibilities relating to student assessment have been incorporated into a principal's expectations (Ministry of Education, Finland, 2007). In general, Finnish principals are responsible for the use of human and financial resources at their schools, for hiring staff members, for organizing their professional development, and for staff evaluation (European Commission, 2024). Teachers in Finland also have a high degree of pedagogical autonomy, with principals trusting teacher professionalism as developers of classroom-level practices and methods. Despite the lack of a specific leadership framework, Finnish principals are known for their strong emphasis on instructional leadership, collaboration with local colleagues, and their ability to adapt to the diverse needs of their school communities; the principal's leadership, whether direct or indirect, influences student learning (Kakon et al., 2014). To support their instructional leadership, all principals have a teaching responsibility beginning at a minimum two hours per week, at a maximum 22 hours per week (Ministry of Education, Finland, 2007).

Ethical leadership in Finland is deeply rooted in the country's cultural and social foundations. As explained in Chap. 4, Finnish educators prioritize ethical principles in their practice. These values include effectiveness and expertise, transparency, trust, impartiality and independence, equality, responsibility, and principles of service. Considering the Shapiro and Stefkovich (2022) framework, the ethic of justice is evident in their treating employees equally and fairly and adhering to laws and cultural norms. "How ethical educational leadership is conducted in Finnish schools is something that school leaders and teachers try to do together" (Hanhimäki & Risku, 2021, p. 87). The ethic of care and ethic of community are also foundational within the Finnish school system. The principle underlying pre-primary, basic, and upper secondary education is to guarantee basic educational security for all, irrespective of their place of residence, language, and economic standing—"Children permanently living in Finland have a statutory right and obligation to complete the comprehensive school syllabus. All children (99.7%) do this" (Ministry of Education, Finland, 2007, p. 13). Finns have confidence in their schooling system, teachers, and principals; and, schooling is seen as a very significant guarantor for the success and well-being of individuals, communities, and the whole society. "Equality is not an empirical but a moral concept. The education system is to be able to rectify societal injustices with positive discrimination. This means that resources and support are directed to where they are needed most" (Hanhimäki & Risku, 2021, p. 88).

In addition to the Comenius' Oath (Trade Union of Education OAJ, 2020), which was previously described in Chap. 4 and applies to all educators in Finland, there are specific ethical standards for Finnish teachers who have a school principal role. In 2014, the Trade Union of Education (OAJ) updated their Code of Ethics for teachers, emphasizing that educational professionals must have both good professional skills and ethical principles, indicating that one could not replace the other. Also in 2018, the Finnish Association of Principals (SURE) developed the Principal's Ethical Code stating that learning and growth is at the core of principal's work. In addition, the code emphasizes the principal's care of the school community and communication between the school community and the Finnish society. "Furthermore, the code underlines equality, respect, encouragement and hope" (Hanhimäki & Risku, 2021, p. 92). The work of the Finnish principal focuses on fostering an ethical educational community in which principals, teachers, and students live well together—and in which students learn how to live well together in the larger community. One principal explained, "The Code of Ethics for Finnish Principals will go with me throughout my leadership career. I will rewrite it in the future so that it will look like me with examples and nuances" (p. 95).

Three ethical principles are evident throughout the Finnish educational system:

> First, striving for equality based on the Nordic welfare state ideology constitutes the fundamental ethical principle on all levels of our educational and societal system. Second, taking care of all individuals in their individual educational and life paths in accordance to their own needs and goals characterizes our system in addition to equality. Third, multi-professional collaboration to support the well-being and development of people of all ages has a long tradition in the Finnish educational system. (Hanhimäki & Risku, 2021, p. 95)

Currently, in Finnish university graduate programs (i.e., the Institute of Educational Leadership at the University of Jyväskylä), principals are provided opportunity for reflective study of leadership ethics as part of their professional development, closely connected with their moral cultural practices of caring, cooperation, respect, commitment, and professionalism.

It is clear that ethical considerations are evident throughout the Finnish education system—and throughout Finnish society. There is also a specific code of ethics for Finnish principals. With their national core curriculum enacted by municipal education authorities, there are not particular province/state/Länder differences in leadership frameworks and governance systems such as those appear in Canada, the United States, and Germany.

"Where the Buck Stops": The Principal's Office

We have worked as principals in a number of Canadian schools, and our consultant and university teaching roles have allowed us to work with a number of American, German, and Finnish principals in professional learning sessions and on-site in their schools. The work of the principal, no matter which country, is challenging, complex, and all-consuming—filled with ethical questions and dilemmas on a daily basis. One of the "double-edged" swords related to ethics, that we have experienced as Canadian principals, is the autonomy that is provided to school principals, either in ministry policy or in district practice. The opportunities to work within a particular learning community developing knowledge and skill together to improve learning for all of our students (obviously, within the constraints of ministry and district frameworks) is work that "lights us up." The difficulty is when values and ethics of other individuals and groups we have worked with collide. Our principal's office was "where the buck stopped," where honest conversations took place, where emotions were sometimes raw, where further inquiry was determined, where difficult decisions were made.

A Canadian Principal: Reflection on Ethical Leadership

Principal Valerie has worked for the school district for many years, starting her career as a teacher and then moving into roles as curriculum coordinator and assistant principal before moving into her current principal role. Her love for early learners and their families provides her "moral imperative" as an ethical leader, and she knows that in this time of limited financial resources for schools every decision she makes has to be in the best interests of her students. She is very aware of the impact of her role as a principal and the visibility that she had within her school community—with her students and parents, with her staff, and with her community partners who provided support for her school programming because of the limited resources of many of her "new Canadian" parents. She is very knowledgeable regarding the expectations of the provincial Principal and Teacher Codes of Conduct; and her view of herself as the "lead teacher" means that she holds herself to a higher standard than she knows some of her principal colleagues or more senior leaders in the district demonstrate.

When I think of ethical leadership, I wonder about leaders who present themselves publicly as an ethical leader and then behave or make decisions that are not consistent with their espoused values. One of the most frustrating things for me as a principal was when I worked with a director who would stand up in meetings and say that all of our work as principals needed be focused on doing what was the "right thing for students." But when, it came to allocating discretionary resources, the money always went to the projects that they could publicly share as "bright and shiny" examples of their own leadership--certainly not acknowledging the importance of developing teaching practice or of improving student outcomes. For me it was an ethical issue, when teaching resources were so badly needed in my school (and in our other schools) for things that should just be basic supplies...I felt that I was forced to take time away from my work with teachers and students to approach local businesses or service clubs for donations to "do the right things" for my students and their families. It was not the "right thing" for me to ask my teachers to use their own money to buy supplies for students or books for their classrooms. It was not right for me to then ask my teachers to buy their own books for a professional learning series when it was mandated by our director...and it was well known amongst our principal group that the director used their corporate credit card to expense elaborate lunches with some of the principals or to send particular principals to expensive out-of-town conferences. I couldn't understand how someone in that important a leadership role could be so self-serving.

As an experienced principal, Valerie is well respected by her colleagues, and her director often asks for her advice regarding early learning pedagogies and what supports are important for elementary schools. Because of her work ethic, commitment to service, and approachable manner, new principals also often come to her to ask the kinds of questions that they would not be comfortable asking their directors. And, she always provides them with advice and connections to available system resources, as well as to her own personal resources. *For me, ethical leadership means having the courage to stay true to my values in how I interact with and provide support for my students and staff members, even if that might be different than some of my principal colleagues or my director.*

An American Principal: Reflection on Ethical Leadership

A large urban high school is a very complex school community to lead, but Principal Marisol thrives on that challenging, vibrant learning environment. Ethical leadership, particularly in the role of a high school principal, is key to shaping the school's culture and the community it serves. *I know that related to leader ethics the [State] standards say that I need to lead my staff to "safely examine" personal assumptions and "respectfully challenge" beliefs that negatively affect improving teaching and learning for all students. But this is also my personal mission. As a child, I remember my abuela telling me that I would be such a great teacher! She so wanted me to have the chance to do the work that she always wanted to do but never was able to because of her family responsibilities and family finances.*

As a female Latino high school principal, she prioritizes ethical decision-making, equity, and social justice. Her leadership is focused on creating an inclusive environment where every student has the opportunity to succeed, regardless of their background. *When I was interviewed and selected for this role, it was quite controversial with my principal peers. They knew I had been a principal in both a middle school and a smaller high school, but this school was viewed as different. A small group of my male high school principal peers even created a "pool" based on how long they thought I would last in this challenging role! Their petty behavior made me determined to outlast them—and to improve the learning environment for my students (and, of course, the teaching environment for my teachers) even more.*

Marisol has been very committed to her work in the [State] Educator Diversity Action Network for a number of years. She also knows that her position as high school principal carries additional ethical responsibility. Her approach aligns with the broader goals of organizations like Latinos for Education, which advocate for increased access and equitable opportunities for Latino students, who make up a significant portion of her student population. She clearly understands the importance of representation and strives to serve as a role model for her students, many of whom may share her cultural heritage. *Although over half of my students are from Latino families, our staff only has a few Latino teachers and support staff. I know that I will really have done my job as an ethical leader when some of our graduates pursue a career in education and will in turn have the opportunity to give back to their community the way that I have been able to.*

As principal, Marisol ensures that all decisions, from resource allocation to disciplinary actions, are made with fairness and the best interests of students at the forefront. Her impact frequently extends beyond the school walls as she works with community boards and task forces, furthering her commitment to community engagement. This engagement is crucial in building trust between her school and the community it serves.

Marisol's ethical leadership is also evident in her dedication to teacher collaboration and professional development, ensuring that her staff is equipped to support the academic success and well-being of each student. She leads by example, demonstrating hard work, self-discipline, and integrity—and encourages her vice-principals and department chairs to do the same in their interactions with students and each other. *I would never ask my staff to do anything that I would not do myself. I know it is so important to "roll up my sleeves" and work alongside them in the really difficult daily work—not just delegating a task and going back to my office.* By promoting a culture of collaboration and inquiry, she listens carefully to the many voices of her staff members and empowers them to work together to address the challenges faced by their diverse student body.

A German Principal: Reflection on Ethical Leadership

In the heart of a bustling German Gemeinschaftsschule school, Principal Herr Schmidt strides confidently, wearing an ensemble resembling that of the early Canadian "Coureurs de Bois." He has just been out in the woods near the school teaching his students survival skills. While there exists no cohesive or explicit legislation in Germany regarding ethical leadership standards for principals, what is clear from our extensive work in Germany is that there is a moral imperative inherent in German educators to act in what we would term ethical ways. Often stereotyped as individuals with stern exteriors and as staunch followers of rules, the German educators, perhaps in response to the tragedies of WWII, are sincere and kindhearted with a strong sense of "doing what is right, in the most right way possible."

Herr Schmidt's belief in a moral purpose is evident in every decision and interaction. For him, ethical leadership is not merely a set of rules to be followed, but a guiding philosophy that shapes the very essence of the educational environment he is working to create. He believes that at the core of ethical leadership lies a commitment to fostering a sense of community and collaboration among both students and faculty. This approach is reflected in the way he values transparency and open communication, ensuring that all stakeholders are involved in decision-making processes. He skillfully creates an atmosphere of trust and shared responsibility—*There are no rules that say I must do this. I just know that this is what my school, my students, and my teachers require.*

Under Herr Schmidt's leadership, ethical considerations extend beyond the academic realm into the broader development of his students as responsible and compassionate individuals. Respect for diversity, inclusivity, and a strong emphasis on moral education are embedded in the curriculum. Each year he asks students to identify the most significant issues they see impacting their school and local community. He then tasks them with developing a real solution to those authentic problems, and he provides them with resources they require to see their solution come to fruition. For example, students were busy installing LCD projectors in each classroom because they identified an issue with poor quality technology in the school. After they had researched the best type of projector and proposed a budget to Herr Schmidt, they examined school building plans to identify the safest location in each room for installation and sought assistance from the school industrial arts teacher to assist them with the tools needed for the installation.

As a school leader I need to show my students how I want them to be in the world. That is my ethical responsibility. I want them to take action and know their voice matters. Maybe we do things differently in my school, but I know my students hold their head high and believe they will make a difference in the world. Herr Schmidt knows that ethical leadership is not a top-down imposition of rules and expected behaviors but a collective effort, where teachers serve as role models, inspiring students to cultivate a strong sense of integrity, empathy, and social responsibility. This shared commitment to ethical principles creates a harmonious and nurturing environment, where every member of the school community plays a role in shaping a future generation of ethical leaders.

A Finnish Principal: Reflection on Ethical Leadership

For those that have closely followed the results of the OECD's PISA test scores, it is no surprise to find Finland has been consistently in the list of top performers, but the "health" of Finnish schools extends far beyond children scoring well on standardized tests of achievement. For Principal

Arto *the health of our Finnish society is a reflection of the health of our education system. Beyond test scores, our 13-year-old PISA test takers express feeling safer in school, report less experience of bullying, and describe a deep sense of belonging in school. For me, the health of the Finnish education system can be "felt" when you walk into a Finnish school. We place such importance on proper schooling for children in Finland—scoring well on tests is not the priority. It is our collective ethical responsibility to foster in children that which will make them good people for this world.*

Principal Arto embodies the core tenets of ethical leadership, emphasizing a philosophy that resonates deeply within his school's ethos. For Arto, ethical leadership is not a prescribed set of rules but a collective organic commitment to fostering a learning community founded on trust, collaboration, and equality. In the Finnish education system, ethical leadership is interwoven into the fabric of daily interactions, where administrators, teachers, and students engage in open dialogue and shared decision-making processes. Arto firmly believes that by creating an atmosphere of respect and cooperation, then ethical leadership by everyone, not just the principal, becomes a guiding force. It allows each member of the school community to thrive and contribute to the collective pursuit of knowledge and personal growth for its young Finnish citizens.

Under Principal Arto's stewardship, ethical leadership for his school community extends beyond a professional obligation and becomes a lived experience—involving his teachers, students, and their families. His emphasis on equity is particularly prominent, with a commitment to providing every student with an inclusive and supportive environment. In Finnish schools, holistic support services are a fundamental aspect of a school's architecture. The expectation is that children and their families, also, must be able to access social services along with mental and physical health supports, easily and consistently, in order to thrive—the school is seen as the best conduit to these supports.

Arto ensures that ethical considerations permeate teaching and learning, fostering a holistic approach to education that nurtures not only academic excellence but also social and emotional well-being. In this way, ethical leadership in Finnish schools becomes a way of being, shaping the values and character of the next generation while fostering a deep sense of responsibility and community engagement. Principal Arto's approach to ethical leadership emphasizes creating a holistic educational experience that not only imparts knowledge but also equips students with the skills and values necessary to navigate an interconnected world with integrity and compassion.

Questions to Consider

- In thinking about the four cultural contexts reflected in this chapter, what might be some of the cultural assumptions or values that you bring to your work as an educational leader?
- How might those considerations related to ethical leadership inform your interactions with principals from other states/provinces and countries?
- How are the various elements of the Shapiro and Stefkovich (2022) multiparadigm framework reflected in each of the country's approaches to ethical principal leadership? Leadership qualifications? Leadership standards or codes of conduct?
- Which of the principal reflections resonated most for you? Why?

Leadership cannot just go along to get along. Leadership must meet the moral challenge of the day.
—Jesse Jackson, American minister, activist, and politician

References

Alberta Education. (2023a). *Leadership quality standard: Ministerial Order #002/2020 (amended 2023)*. https://open.alberta.ca/publications/leadership-quality-standard

Alberta Education. (2023b). *Superintendent leadership quality standard: Ministerial Order #0203/2020 (amended 2023)*. https://open.alberta.ca/publications/superintendent-leadership-quality-standard

BC Principal's & Vice-Principal's Association. (2019). *BCPVPA leadership standards for principals and vice-principals in BC*. https://bcpvpa.insite.com/files/assets/83/bcpvpaleadershipstandardsjuly2019.pdf

California Commission on Teacher Credentialing. (2014). *California professional standards for educational leaders* (CPSEL). https://www.ctc.ca.gov/docs/default-source/educator-prep/standards/cpsel-booklet-2014.pdf

Doan, B., & Jaber, L. (2021). HERLeadership: Addressing the continued lack of women in leadership. *Journal of Leadership, Accountability and Ethics, 18*(5), 1–9. https://doi.org/10.33423/jlae.v18i5

European Commission. (2023). *National education systems—Germany: Administration and governance.* https://eurydice.eacea.ec.europa.eu/national-education-systems/germany/administration-and-governance-local-andor-institutional-level

European Commission. (2024). *National education systems—Finland: Administration and governance.* https://eurydice.eacea.ec.europa.eu/national-education-systems/finland/administration-and-governance-local-andor-institutional-level

Government of Alberta. (2024). *Teaching code of professional conduct.* https://www.alberta.ca/code-of-professional-conduct

Hancock, D., Müller, U., Wang, C., & Hachen, J. (2019). Factors influencing school principals' motivation to become principals in the U.S.A. and Germany. *International Journal of Educational Research, 95*, 90–96. https://doi.org/10.1016/j.ijer.2019.04.004

Hanhimäki, E., & Risku, M. (2021). The cultural and social foundations of ethical educational leadership in Finland. In R. Normand, L. Moos, M. Liu, & P. Tulowitzki (Eds.), *The cultural and social foundations of educational leadership* (Educational governance research) (Vol. 16). Springer. https://doi.org/10.1007/978-3-030-74497-7_5

Jantunen, A., Ahtiainen, R., Lahtero, T., & Kallioniemi, A. (2022). Finnish comprehensive school principals' descriptions of diversity in their school communities. *International Journal of Leadership in Education*, 1–21. https://doi.org/10.1080/13603124.2022.2117416

Kakon, S., Halttunen, L., & Pekke, K. (2014). Sources of principals' leadership practices and areas training should emphasize: Case Finland. *Journal of Leadership Education, 13*(2), 29–51. https://doi.org/10.12806/V13/I2/R2

Klein, E., & Bronnert-Härle, H. (2020). Mature school cultures and new leadership practices: An analysis of leadership for learning in German comprehensive schools. *Z Erziehungswiss, 23*, 955–977. https://doi.org/10.1007/s11618-020-00968-4

Klein, E. D., & Schwanenberg, J. (2022). Ready to lead school improvement? Perceived professional development needs of principals in Germany. *Educational Management Administration & Leadership, 50*(3), 371–391. https://doi.org/10.1177/1741143220933901

Lahtero, T., Ahtiainen, R., & Lång, N. (2019). Finnish principals: Leadership training and views on distributed leadership. *Education Research and Reviews, 14*(10), 340–348. https://doi.org/10.5897/ERR2018.3637

Ministry of Education, Finland. (2007). *Improving school leadership, Finland: Country background report.* http://www.oecd.org/education/preschoolandschool/38529249.pdf

National Center on Education and the Economy. (2017). *Germany: Teacher and principal quality.* https://ncee.org/country/germany/

National Center on Education and the Economy. (2023). *Finland: Teachers and principals.* https://ncee.org/country/finland/

National Policy Board for Educational Administration. (2015). *Professional standards for educational leaders.* https://www.npbea.org/wp-content/uploads/2017/06/Professional-Standards-for-Educational-Leaders_2015.pdf

Ontario College of Teachers. (2024). *Ethical standards.* https://www.oct.ca/public/professional-standards/ethical-standards

Ontario Institute for Educational Leadership. (2013). *Ontario leadership framework.* https://www.education-leadership-ontario.ca/application/files/8814/9452/4183/Ontario_Leadership_Framework_OLF.pdf

Ontario Institute for Educational Leadership. (2024a). *Strategic plan.* https://www.education-leadership-ontario.ca/en/about/strategic-plan

Ontario Institute for Educational Leadership. (2024b). *Deepening the implementation of the Ontario Leadership Framework (OLF).* https://www.education-leadership-ontario.ca/en/resources/ontario-leadership-framework-olf/deepening-implementation-olf

Sekretariat der Kultusministerkonferenz. (2004). *Standards für die Lehrerbildung: Bildungswissenschaften.* https://www.kmk.org/fileadmin/veroeffentlichungen_beschluesse/2004/2004_12_16-Standards-Lehrerbildung-Bildungswissenschaften.pdf

Shapiro, J., & Stefkovich, J. (2022). *Ethical leadership and decision making in education: Applying theoretical perspectives to complex dilemmas* (5th ed.). https://doi.org/10.4324/9781003022862

Trade Union of Education OAJ. (2020). *Comenius' oath for teachers.* https://www.oaj.fi/en/education/ethical-principles-of-teaching/comenius-oath-for-teachers/

Tulowitzki, P., Hinzen, I., & Roller, M. (2019). The qualifications of school principals in Germany: A nationwide overview. *DDS—The German School, 111*(2), 149–169. https://doi.org/10.31244/dds.2019.02.04

York Region District School Board. (2020). *Leadership framework for school administrators.* https://www.yrdsb.ca/Careers/Documents/YRDSB_Leadership_Framework_School_Admins.pdf

CHAPTER 6

Leadership Lessons from Toxic Educational Workplace Cultures

Abstract In this chapter, we provide examples of what have been described to us by educators as their experiences with unethical leadership in toxic school and school district cultures. The examples in this chapter include educators who are from three different levels in the typical hierarchy of school districts—teachers, principals, and superintendents/directors. (We know that toxic employee behavior in schools and school districts impacts teachers in a significant way—and educators who have formal leadership designations are also not immune to those negative impacts.) Each example includes a vignette of their experience, as well as their reflections on the impacts of the unethical leadership behavior and toxic workplace culture on their productivity and wellness, on their students, and on school district effectiveness and credibility in their larger communities. Each of the examples also includes questions for reader reflection.

Keywords Vignettes of leadership practice • Educator voices • Toxic school cultures • Emotional contagion • Impact of unethical educational leadership

> "It's also our collective delusion that overwork and burnout are the prices we must pay in order to succeed."
> —Arianna Huffington, *Greek American author, syndicated columnist, and businesswoman*

© The Author(s), under exclusive license to Springer Nature Switzerland AG 2024
B. Yee, D. Yee, *International Perspectives on Ethical Educational Leadership*, https://doi.org/10.1007/978-3-031-70839-8_6

In Chap. 2 we provided an overview of the organizational psychology literature regarding healthy and toxic workplace cultures. We also explored healthy and toxic school cultures, considering literature related to the possible impacts of unethical leadership and toxic cultures on staff member wellness, on employee development and productivity, and on student learning outcomes—as well as parent and community perceptions of school system effectiveness. In this chapter, we provide examples of what have been described to us by educators as their experiences with unethical leadership in toxic school and school district cultures. We know that toxic employee behavior in schools and school districts impacts teachers in a significant way—and educators who have formal leadership designations are not immune to those negative impacts. The examples in this chapter, and in Chap. 7, include educators who are from three different levels in the typical hierarchy of school districts—teachers, principals, and superintendents/directors. Each example includes a vignette of their experience, as well as their reflections on the impacts of the unethical leadership behavior and toxic workplace culture on their productivity and wellness, on their students, and on school district effectiveness and credibility in their larger communities. Each of the examples also includes questions for reader reflection.

Toxic Workplace Cultures

To begin this chapter for readers who may not have read Chap. 2 and to also provide connection to that chapter, we have included a brief overview and two additional frames (i.e., Epitropoulos, 2019; Sutton, 2010) to assist with reader reflection on the leadership vignettes in this chapter. In Chap. 2 we introduced readers to Bob Sutton, an organizational psychologist and Stanford professor who studies and writes about leadership, navigating organizational life, and organizational change. To illustrate the pervasiveness of toxic workplace cultures, Sutton's (2010) experience of candidly writing about the negative behavior of individuals and groups and their impact on whole organizations prompted a flood of responses from "people in all kinds of jobs from all around the world" (p. 4) questioning why they had put up with this behavior for so long without taking concrete steps to stop the behavior:

> Whatever these creeps are called, many of them are clueless about their behavior. Even worse, some of them are proud of it. Other jerks are trou-

bled and embarrassed by their behavior but can't seem to contain or control their meanness. All are similar, however, in that they infuriate, demean and damage their peers, superiors, underlings, and at times clients and customers, too. (p. 5)

Organizational development and psychology professors Mitchell Kusy and Elizabeth Holloway from Antioch University (2009) have studied the impact of toxic employees with 400 business leaders, many from the Fortune 500 list. They found that 94% of those leaders reported working with a toxic employee within the past five years and 64% reported that they were currently working with a toxic individual, describing it as "incivility that runs rampant in the workplace today" (Kusy, 2018b, p. 1). The leaders in the study described the impact of toxic employees on their personal well-being and on their own performance, as well as the performance of their team and organization. Kusy (2018a) also highlights the significant financial impact to organizations of allowing toxic employee behavior.

In further explaining the psychology of toxic workplace cultures, Sutton (2017) describes the notion of "emotional contagion" and explains that employee emotions, including anger, contempt, and fear, are very contagious even for other employees who observe negative language and behavior. "In conversation, people tend automatically and continuously to mimic and synchronize their movements with the facial expressions, voices postures, movements, and instrumental behaviors of others" (p. 93). Sutton explains that contagion studies also show that "when people 'catch' unpleasant expressions from others, like frowning or glaring it makes them feel grumpier and angrier—even though they don't realize or deny that it is happening to them" (p. 95). Sutton indicates that if positive, ethical, and respectful individuals are hired into a team with "self-centred nasty, narrow-minded unethical or overworked or physically ill [colleagues], there is little chance that [one individual] will turn them into better human beings or transform it into a healthy workplace—even a tiny company" (p. 95). These findings, and our own experiences in schools and school districts, make us ask questions about the transformational leadership literature which often describes the power of leaders to engage with followers to foster ethical decision-making, moral action, and an ethical group climate or culture (Northouse, 2022).

Organizational psychology scholars and researchers generally have studied business workplaces. In this chapter, our vignettes consider unethical leadership and toxic workplace culture "in the trenches/on the front lines" of schools and school districts. (The phrases "in the trenches" and "on the front lines" are language from the educators whose voices are represented in this chapter, to indicate the depth of emotion involved).

Toxic School and School District Cultures

Recently professional discussions related to toxic school cultures have begun to gain more prominence. Epitropoulos (2019) summarized ten signs of a toxic school culture based on a presentation by Robyn Jackson at the Association for Supervision and Curriculum Development Empower19 conference. Jackson, a former teacher and school administrator who is now CEO of Mindsteps Inc.®, has published a number of books on educational leadership, teacher professional learning, and student engagement. As previously indicated, the principal is typically positioned as the key agent in establishing and sustaining an ethical culture in their school: "The process of overhauling values, mission, and vision is healing in and of itself. When you shape your work around these things, you will change your [school] culture—and leave no room for toxicity to grow" (para. 16).

Epitropoulos (2019) summarized ten warning signs of a toxic school culture:

1. No clear sense of purpose—If school administrators and teachers don't share a common goal, they will work toward their own agenda which will eventually create conflict.
2. Hostile relations among staff, students, and parents—When elephants fight, it's the grass that suffers. When the adults in the room fight, no one can focus well on the most important thing: the students.
3. An emphasis on rules over people or mission—This issue is often created at the district level. Teachers are more focused on the rules than on serving students and feel they have little latitude to do their jobs.
4. An absence of honest dialogue—Principals who avoid difficult conversations with teachers and address issues by reassigning the teacher or changing a teacher's schedule aren't truly serving kids.
5. More self-preservation than collaboration—When self-preservation takes priority over serving kids, it's difficult for good ideas and talented teachers to stick around.

6. Active back channels over formal lines of communication—If more is being said and accomplished in unofficial meetings after the staff meeting, it's a sign that teachers don't trust each other. If the rumor mill controls everything, it leaves an opening for people to make their own narratives. Whoever controls the narrative controls school culture.
7. Punishment instead of recognition, and rewards and behavior motivated by the avoidance of punishment—If colleagues punish bad behavior and don't reward good behavior, the culture encourages students and staff to do the minimum to avoid getting punished, but not to excel.
8. A palpable lack of safety—If people are afraid to speak up, they can't address problems head on. When teachers aren't free to be vulnerable, they don't feel safe in uncomfortable conversations.
9. A small group who controls the conversation—If a few dominant voices control the culture of your school, toxicity thrives. It's imperative to find ways to help everyone speak up.
10. An absence of risk taking—People are afraid to do what they feel is right for kids because they're afraid to step away from the pack. If teachers try nothing new, the kids are the ones who suffer. (para. 2–11)

Based on our review of current research and our experience as teachers and leaders in K-12 schools, we would suggest that these warning signs are accurate. We ask readers to consider which of these indicators are present in the vignettes of educators' experiences with toxic school and school district cultures.

Sutton (2010) also provides a helpful, albeit "cheeky," framework to consider these vignettes of unethical educational leadership and toxic school cultures. Using candid language, he presents his "Top 10 Steps—Enforcing the No Asshole Rule" based on numerous research studies from his academic colleagues in organizational psychology and workplace dynamics, as well as his own research and interactions with teams and whole organizations:

- Say the rule, write it down, and act on it—But if you can't or don't follow the rule, it is better to say nothing at all; avoiding a false claim is the lesser of two evils. You don't want to be known as a hypocrite and the leader of an organization that is filled with assholes.

- Assholes will hire assholes—Keep your resident jerks out of the hiring process, or if you can't, involve as many 'civilized' people in interviews and decisions to offset this predilection of people to hire 'jerks like me.'
- Get rid of assholes fast—Organizations usually wait too long to get rid of certified and incorrigible assholes, and once they do, the reaction is usually, 'Why did we wait so long to do that?'
- Treat certified assholes as incompetent employees—Even if people do other things extraordinarily well but persistently demean others, they ought to be treated as incompetent.
- Power breeds nastiness—Beware that giving people—even seemingly nice and sensitive people—even a little power can turn them into big jerks.
- Embrace the power-performance paradox—Accept that your organization does have and should have a pecking order but do everything you can to downplay and reduce unnecessary status differences among members. The result will be fewer assholes and, according to the best studies, better performance, too.
- Manage moments—not just practices, policies, and systems—Effective asshole management means focusing on and changing the little things that you and your people do—and big changes will follow. Reflect on what you do, watch how others respond to you and to one another, and work on 'tweaking' what happens as you are interacting with the person in front of you right now.
- Model and teach constructive confrontation—Develop a culture where people know when to argue and when to stop fighting and, instead, gather more evidence, listen to other people, or stop whining and implement a decision (even if they still disagree with it.) When the time is ripe to battle over ideas, follow Karl Weick's advice; fight as if you are right; listen as if you are wrong.
- Adopt the one asshole rule—Because people follow rules and norms better when there are rare or occasional examples of bad behavior, no asshole rules might be most closely followed in organizations that permit one or two token jerks to hang around. These 'reverse role models' remind everyone else of the wrong behavior.
- The bottom line: link big policies to small decencies—Effective asshole management happens when there is a virtuous, self-reinforcing cycle between the 'big' things that organizations do and the little

things that happen when people talk to one another and work together. (pp. 87–89)

When reading the vignettes which follow, we also ask readers to consider which of Sutton's "Steps" (or remedies) school-based and district-based leaders might adopt to improve the situation described.

As we explained in Chap. 1, these leadership vignettes include educators holding a variety of positions in K-12 schools and school districts which are culturally rich with many ethnicities, faiths, and gender perspectives represented. Because of this diversity, we have used "they" as well as the "he/she" gender specific pronouns. And, we have used given names which are representative of the diversity of these school communities. In the vignettes, the text in italics represents the particular language of the educator.

ONE TEACHER'S EXPERIENCE

When my previous principal left the school to move to another city, I was really nervous about who we would get as a new principal. I loved working with that principal, following them to this school from the school where I previously worked as a curriculum leader. As I left the meeting with this new principal, I knew that I would have to leave this school where I had developed positive relationships with many staff members and parents (and where my son attended) if I wanted an opportunity to be part of the leadership development cohort in the system—and to someday achieve my goal of becoming a school principal. If and when that day happened, I vowed I would never treat my staff members the way this principal treated me.

Alejandro was a mid-career teacher who had a number of years of successful experience in the school district, after growing up and being trained as a teacher in the United Kingdom. He had emigrated to Canada, married a police officer, and were now raising a young family, with three children in elementary school—the eldest in the same school where Alejandro worked. Alejandro had a number of conversations about graduate school with the previous principal who had just completed her doctorate in educational leadership. It was exciting for Alejandro to think about the challenge of completing a graduate degree. Also, in order to apply for principal positions in the district, Alejandro knew that teachers had to have a master's degree.

Alejandro was a curriculum leader with the previous principal. That leadership team had provided a very dynamic environment where curriculum leaders who were very passionate about learning and leadership shared innovative ideas, journal articles, and innovative teaching strategies—and had honest, and often blunt, conversations about improving learning for their students. Then they worked with their teacher groups to put the new strategies in place and gather evidence of improved student learning. It had been wonderful to see students who had previously struggled begin to show that they could be confident learners. Alejandro knew that this type of leadership work was something that he wanted to do long term. Working with the previous principal and being part of that school leadership team had allowed Alejandro to begin developing his leadership skills. He enrolled in a master's degree program and successfully completed it the summer before the new principal arrived.

When the new principal began work at the school, it was clear that he was used to doing things quite differently in the school that he came from, even though it was in the same district. Because curriculum leader positions in the school district were annual appointments in their collective agreement, the new principal knew he could remove the curriculum leader positions from the previous year. He created different expectations for a smaller number of positions with emphasis on management tasks versus the instructional leadership focus of the previous leadership team. When Alejandro was not a successful applicant for one of the new positions, he asked to meet with the new principal to discuss what he needed to do to be part of the school leadership team in the future.

In order to apply for a vice-principal position, teachers needed to be part of leadership development cohort and attend monthly professional development sessions. Each year approximately 40 teachers were admitted into the VP leadership cohort from a group of over 150 initial applicants. It was a complicated application process with points being assessed for graduate course work and program completion, conference presentations given, articles written, languages spoken, previous school-based leadership roles, and so forth. Applicants who met the initial screening criteria needed to do an academic presentation for a group of principals. And from there, a smaller group would complete an interview with trios of system senior leaders to reduce the applicants pool to the cohort of 40. (A similar cohort system was in place for vice-principals who wanted to be principals.) However, to start the cohort application process, the applicant's principal needed to sign the form saying that they believed the applicant was "ready to be a vice-principal." So, the applicant's principal was the gatekeeper to leadership development in the district.

Alejandro spent a lot of time preparing for the meeting with the new principal because at the same time he needed to ask the principal to sign the application package for the vice-principal cohort in order to meet the system deadline. Alejandro really wanted the principal to understand what important and challenging work he had done through his Master of Educational Leadership program and how he had envisioned helping the teachers at the school improve their practice. Alejandro's university professors had provided very positive feedback on his work, and he had received all A's in his courses. One professor had even suggested that Alejandro publish his work in a national journal on educational leadership.

The day of the meeting, the principal was returning to the school from another meeting, and their meeting started 15 minutes late. It became obvious to Alejandro that the principal was not really interested in learning more about his previous leadership work at the school or his graduate studies. When Alejandro approached the subject of a future curriculum leader role and the vice-principal cohort application, the principal appeared quite uncomfortable and mumbled that his director had expected them to reorganize the school leadership structure and that there was not enough money in the school budget to purchase the previous numbers of curriculum leaders. When Alejandro, asked for the principal's signature on his vice-principal application, the principal said that he didn't know enough about Alejandro's work to sign the application for this year's cohort but possibly would sign it next year. The conversation ended with the principal indicating that he was very excited to have Alejandro lead the professional development committee and to coach the boys' basketball team and soccer teams just like last year.

Alejandro later learned from the school "rumor mill" that the current vice-principal who was very traditional in his approach to teaching and who had struggled with the innovative approaches of the previous principal had told new principal that Alejandro was "a favorite" of the previous principal. And, that the new principal had already signed off on one of the vice-principal's friends' applications for the cohort.

The Teacher's Reflections

On Staff Member Wellness, as Well as Employee Development and Productivity

In the teacher's vignette, employee development and productivity are the key issues. *How can I give my best to my students, when I feel like I am always "looking over my shoulder" to see how the new principal and vice-principal are looking at my work or talking about me to other staff? I love my work in the classroom, but I also want to develop my leadership skills and work to my goal of being a school principal someday. I know the previous principal and my university professors saw the leader in me.* Alejandro knew that this toxic environment was not good for him emotionally, and he sought advice from the teacher association. The teacher association representative was empathetic and offered association counselling. The representative also suggested that Alejandro apply to teach and be a curriculum leader in another school because this issue was common to certain principals in the district.

On Student Learning Outcomes

What motivated Alejandro the most about working on the leadership team of the previous principal was that the focus of the group was leading teacher and student learning. They had a reduced teaching load because of their leadership role, but it was clear that they were selected as master teachers in their subject discipline. And, they met regularly to discuss the student work they were observing in the classrooms—and student project and test results. One of Alejandro's children, Carlos, had a learning disability, and Alejandro worked with Carlos at home to help him with his schoolwork. Alejandro saw from a parent's perspective what a difference it made for Carlos' learning and emotional health when teachers used the universal design for learning and backward design approaches that their leadership team were helping teachers use in the classroom. With the very traditional "sit and get" and "pull out resource" approaches that the new principal was comfortable with, Alejandro worried about all students—but Carlos, in particular.

On Parent and Community Perceptions of School District Effectiveness

When Alejandro moved to the city and began looking for teaching jobs, he had asked his neighbors about the school district. People in the community said that some schools had great teachers but that they "needed to watch out" for the organization's leadership and be very cautious about who their principal might be. Police colleagues of Alejandro's spouse who worked closely with the schools also mentioned the school principals and how they felt some principals were great and some were "really into creating kingdoms" in their schools.

Most importantly, Alejandro realized that he had been placed in "lose-lose" situation by the new principal and that the principal actually enjoyed the ability to be the gatekeeper for leadership development opportunities in the district and "giving out those favors" to gain further control or social capital.

Questions to Consider

- How does the ethic of justice apply to this situation?
- How does the ethic of care relate to this leadership vignette? How might it hinder or support the ethic of justice?
- Thinking about the Shapiro and Stefkovich multiparadigm framework (2022), how does the ethic of the profession inform this vignette?
- Was it ethical for the principal to remove all of the curriculum leader designations and reconfigure the leadership team? Or to tell Alejandro that they couldn't sign the vice-principal application this year but might possibly sign it next year?
- Which of the signs of a toxic work culture were evident in this vignette?
- Which of Sutton's remedies might leaders consider to improve this workplace culture?

ONE PRINCIPAL'S EXPERIENCE

As I hung up from the Zoom call, I couldn't believe what I had just endured! I was expecting to meet with my superintendent for a quick "return to work Zoom meeting" following a medical leave from my work as principal. It was the middle of the Covid-19 pandemic, and schools had just begun operating on a remote learning platform. I was eager to return to the school to help my staff adjust to this work context that was so different from their typical work. While I was away, a number of my staff had been calling and texting me asking for my help because they knew how comfortable I was using technology in teaching and learning. What actually happened in the meeting was an ambush from my superintendent and an HR advisor where I was told to leave the call and return with my principal's association representative. Before I could call my representative, I received an email which was sent to all school staff by the acting principal, who also was a personal friend of the superintendent, indicating that my medical leave had been extended until the end of the year. What the $!#% was going on? I called my association rep who said that they didn't have any details. We both logged into the Zoom call. The HR advisor then told us that there had been complaints about my work as a principal and I would be unassigned from duties until the complaints were investigated. Then, I knew the reason that the superintendent had been going to my school numerous times while I was on medical leave, running staff meetings and berating my staff for "bad behavior", and asking my school secretary peculiar questions about school finances. My superintendent was "giving me a spanking" because as a new principal I had been very vocal in supporting my staff to resolve a decade long issue with a toxic school building that had caused serious medical issues for more than 20 of my staff members! And, the impact of the building on my immune system was the reason I had gone on my medical leave. I was shaking with anger as I picked up the phone and called my association rep back to debrief the meeting.

Elle had worked for the school district a number of years in a variety of school-based and district roles before becoming a principal—an award-winning classroom teacher, curriculum leader in several schools, system specialist for technology, and very successful assistant principal in several schools. Elle's peers and supervisors knew Elle for her skill and passion for engaging students and staff members in innovative teaching practice and experiential learning, often including technology. When Elle moved into the principalship, she replaced a principal who had been at the school for over a decade. Immediately staff members came to Elle to ask her to fix a number of issues that had been long ignored by the previous principal. Within the first few months of the principalship, Elle was dealing with a school secretary who had alcohol addiction issues and a "near miss" between her vehicle and a student in the school parking lot. Shortly after that, several female staff members disclosed that the technology assistant had made inappropriate sexual comments and advances to them.

Elle knew proper system process and protocol and had contacted her superintendent for advice on how to proceed with these complex personnel issues. The superintendent was a long-term personal friend and "golf buddy" of the previous principal and initially reassured Elle that the staff were "just blowing the issues out of proportion." As Elle did further investigation of her own, she found that the staff member complaints were well founded and believed they needed to be addressed. Elle pursued these issues and solved them on her own without further assistance from the superintendent.

What was most concerning to staff members was the condition of the school building which staff members believed was the cause of a number of long-term staff member illnesses, particularly among female staff. When Elle approached the superintendent about the building issues, the superintendent indicated that they had worked with the superintendent of building services, the superintendent of maintenance, and the previous principal—and that there was a building modernization planned in the future. Elle did not believe that was a "good enough" response for their current staff members, students, and parents.

In the second year at the school, Elle began to experience immune system issues similar to her long-term staff. Two excellent staff members had left the school because of deteriorating health, and there were numerous short-term medical leaves. One new staff member began to develop serious symptoms during her first year at the school. Elle hesitated to take any time away from the school to attend to her health because of worries for their staff wellness. She started planning staff professional development activities related to wellness using her own personal funds—because there were no funds available from the district, when Elle inquired.

From previous work in other schools, Elle had developed a very positive relationship with the superintendent of maintenance. With Elle's superintendent unwilling to support a more proactive approach to the building issues, Elle approached that superintendent with staff member concerns. The superintendent of maintenance responded to Elle's request and came to the school to assess the building condition. That superintendent was also very concerned about the building which had mold and mildew problems, carbon monoxide issues, and aging/faulty air handling and heating equipment. The superintendent of maintenance began to remediate what was possible within the scope of the maintenance department. Clearly the building needed far more work to make it healthy for students and staff members, and the superintendent of maintenance continued to work directly with Elle. It was common during this time for Elle to spend a great deal of the school day working with maintenance staff and managing student learning and staff teaching around workmen in hazmat suits.

The staff told Elle they were very angry with and had "absolutely no trust" in the previous superintendent who they explained had rushed by staff members collapsed on the ground in a previous school evacuation due to carbon monoxide to get to their vehicle and speed away. A large group of the long-term staff had hired lawyers related to the inaction of the previous principal and previous superintendent regarding the concerns they had expressed about the health of the building. In the spring of the second year, Elle asked to have the whole staff meeting with members from the superintendent's office as well as the maintenance department and the building services department. Elle also asked to have a representative from the teachers' and principals' associations attend because of how contentious the issue had become. The meeting became very heated, and Elle received little support from her superintendent.

Elle's previous superintendent moved to a different position, and a new superintendent who had also worked for the building services department was appointed. The new superintendent was initially very positive about the innovative and impactful work that Elle was doing at the school to improve teaching practice and student learning and had even asked Elle to present the work of her students and teachers at a school board meeting.

By January of the third year, Elle's doctor indicated that she needed to take a medical leave to help rebuild her immune system away from the toxic school building. On the last day of school before Elle's medical leave was to begin, there was a second whole staff meeting for an update on building issues. The meeting was attended by the new superintendent and the incoming acting principal. Again, personnel from the maintenance department and the building services department attended, as well as representatives from the teachers' and principals' associations. This again became a very heated meeting where the PowerPoint graphs and charts from building services personnel minimized the building issues and served to inflame staff members. Following the meeting, the new superintendent scolded Elle in front of the incoming acting principal and the HR advisor for not supporting senior leaders and "not controlling her staff better."

When the district moved to online learning several weeks later because of the COVID-19 pandemic, the principal called the superintendent for an update because staff members had been reaching out to Elle for assistance. The conversation started with the superintendent saying "I'm so $!#% pissed off at you!" and ended as a 90-minute verbal harangue with inappropriate and inaccurate statements about Elle's leadership at the school and the work of Elle's staff members. Elle was in tears and told the superintendent that the call had damaged their previously positive relationship. The next time Elle had any contact from the superintendent was in the Zoom "return to work" call.

The Principal's Reflections

On Staff Member Wellness

In this principal's vignette, staff member wellness is a primary issue, both physical and emotional wellness. Prior to this principal's arrival, the school had experienced the traumatic event of a former student returning to the school with a weapon attempting to harm the principal and some of the staff members. When Elle arrived, it was clear to her (having worked on the district crisis team) that there were long-term impacts on individuals and groups within the staff because they had not healed from that traumatic event. Those emotional health issues impacted how staff reacted to the issues presented by the unhealthy, aging building. The principal contacted district crisis team personnel for advice; and, when Elle showed the staff that she believed in and supported them, staff members began to trust and support the principal. The emotional healing had just begun when this incident occurred.

On Employee Development and Productivity

The toxic workplace culture that Elle described illustrates the serious physical and emotional impact of unethical leadership practices on staff member development and productivity. Staff absences and medical leaves, both short and long term, were typical in the school when Elle arrived. Staff members had not engaged in the professional learning that other school staff members in the district had experienced and that contributed to the very traditional teaching practices present in the school. Teachers had not been challenged and supported to grow as professionals in a long time, and Elle knew their teachers needed to comply with recently updated teaching standards. Teacher development became a key priority in the principal's work.

On Student Learning Outcomes

When I became a principal, I thought that I would be able to be an even better instructional leader than I had been as an assistant principal or a system specialist. What actually happened was that in this school, there were so many personnel and building issues to deal with that I was often taken away from my instructional leadership work, which is mandated in our principal leadership standard. On top of that, there were so many meetings that I was required to attend, called by my superintendent and other system leaders, that I was not able to spend the time in the school that I needed to focus on improving student learning.

On Parent and Community Perceptions of School District Effectiveness
In their district, Elle explained that parent perceptions of the district were not generally positive, believing the district was "top-heavy" and out of touch with what was happening in the community. Perceptions of the effectiveness of the local schools often depended on how well the principals marketed their school achievement and student programming to the community. When Elle spoke with the director of the school district about the legal issue that was brewing because of unethical leader behavior related to the toxic building, she was told by the director to make sure the issue "was kept out of the newspaper."

Most importantly, Elle learned the lengths that some school districts and unethical district leaders will go to "cover up" issues impacting employee wellness rather than admitting that there is a problem (which is already obvious to many people in the district) and correcting the issue in an effective manner.

Questions to Consider

- How does the ethic of care apply to this situation?
- How does the ethic of justice relate to this leadership vignette? How might it hinder or support caring for employees in situations like the COVID-19 pandemic?
- Thinking about the Shapiro and Stefkovich multiparadigm framework (2022), how does the ethic of the profession apply to this vignette?
- Was it ethical for the principal to seek out further support for the health and well-being of her staff members when her superintendent was not willing to be supportive?
- Which of the signs of a toxic work culture were evident in this vignette?
- Which of Sutton's remedies might leaders consider to improve this workplace culture?

One Associate Director's Experience

As I left the Director's office with my letter of reprimand in a closed manila envelope, I knew that I could no longer work for this person who led my school district so ineffectively. Mixed emotions—biting anger; sadness and a sense of personal and professional loss; incredulity at the realization that, after nearly 20 years working for the district and moving from school principal to several superintendent roles and now associate director, I could be treated so poorly.

Chen had moved to the large urban school district after working as a teacher, counsellor, and principal in several other school districts. An award-winning principal, he was hired into a very complex high school principal role—after a national search which was not typical of the organization. The clear expectation from hiring superintendents was that Chen would lead the huge high school out of a negative staff culture, low student achievement, and financial difficulties during a time of significant ministry and district change regarding high school programming. Following a number of years as a successful principal, he was approached by senior leaders to join the superintendent cohort. Chen moved upward in the system hierarchy in the 15 years that followed—a system principal position, a system superintendent of inclusionary practice, and a superintendent of schools and programs. And, he had been encouraged by the new director to apply for a newly created associate director position in a system leadership reorganization.

Within the district, there was a small group of individuals who had gone to the district schools as students, had been hired as teachers, and had moved up through the hierarchy to principal positions. One of this group had applied for the principal job that Chen was hired into as an external candidate. Through the years in the system, Chen had been invited into or been the successful applicant for several roles and positions that this group also aspired to, including the new associate director position. During the years working with this group as principal and superintendent peers, Chen had been subject to a number of attempts to damage his credibility. In fact, the group was widely known to many people inside and outside the district as the "Gang" because of their dislike for and attempts to discredit anyone who they thought would hamper their possibilities of becoming superintendents. They were also skilled at grooming a small group of followers who often performed "their dirty work." In the new role of associate director, Chen became the direct supervisor of two of this group.

When hired as associate director, Chen had explained the difficulties he had experienced through the years because of this group to both the new director and the new HR associate director who indicated that they "would manage it and that [Chen] didn't need to be concerned."

Within a week of the district announcement that Chen was the new associate director, an email was sent to the director, and including the legal department, human resources, and other superintendents, accusing Chen of unprofessional conduct. The sender pretended to be a parent, but by the language peculiarities and tone of the email, Chen recognized that the author was one of the "Gang." Chen responded with a terse email to the "Gang" colleague, who was posing as a parent, indicating that he was expecting the ongoing harassment to stop and that he had contacted his personal lawyer. In a follow-up email to the director and to Chen, the "Gang" colleague said that they were not a parent and had disguised their identity because they were concerned about retribution from Chen. The director then emailed Chen to set up a meeting to deal with his response. During the meeting the director indicated that they needed to investigate this anonymous complaint. Chen explained that previous directors in the district had never responded to complaints of this nature which were anonymous and appeared malicious—and in this case, designed to discredit a competent employee. It became obvious that the director was very concerned about his reputation, having already sent a follow-up email to the "Gang fake parent" to indicate he did not approve of Chen's email. The meeting, as Chen described it, was attended by the HR associate director to "take notes" and assist the director in delivering a disciplinary message and letter which had been crafted by the HR associate director. It was not a meeting to hear any of Chen's perspectives.

What made me the most disgusted was that at the end of the meeting the Director and the HR Associate Director both told me that this letter of reprimand would not be put on my employee file but would be kept in their desk drawers because of my senior leadership role in the organization. I felt this was a threatening gesture and was certain they would not have treated my other senior leader colleagues in the same way. I had many years' experience dealing with complex discipline and competency issues involving educators—and I would never have treated any of these employees with such disrespect, disregard, and lack of "due process." I found the numbers for my director's association, my lawyer, and prepared my notes for those calls.

The Associate Director's Reflections

On Staff Member Wellness
Chen had experienced the professional and personal impacts of the harassment by this group of colleagues for many years. When Chen had discussed the issue with confidantes, they identified the notion of him being a "tall poppy" and a target for harassment by jealous colleagues. Chen had been a school counsellor early in his career and had a graduate degree in psychology. Generally, Chen felt emotionally equipped to deal with such petty behavior and just kept working hard for the district, either ignoring or directly confronting the "Gang" colleagues when they made derogatory comments in his presence. Chen had spoken with his previous supervisors about the harassment issues; they were supportive and attempted to mediate or stop the inappropriate behavior. And, Chen continued to be very well respected by the principals and teachers he worked with and supervised.

On Employee Development and Productivity
After nearly 20 years of putting up with this nonsense from my colleagues, I had become so tired of the mean spiritedness, laziness, and entitled behavior that was impacting me and a number of other talented, hard-working, and sincere educators in the district. I was tired of always feeling that I had to watch my back around this group, and I knew I needed to respond in a very clear way to their unethical behavior. As an associate director in the district, if I couldn't stand up to this group, who could.

On Student Learning Outcomes
Almost every school district has a mission or goal explicitly stating that they are focused on improving student learning and providing the best educational experience possible for every student. *When I was spending any of my time focusing on the harassment and unethical behavior that impacted me or other district employees, that was time that I was not able to focus on student learning—our organizational purpose. What a huge waste of public funds which we had promised to carefully steward for our community!*

On Parent and Community Perceptions of School District Effectiveness
In general, parents indicated that they were positive about what their teachers and principals did for students in their community schools but expressed negative perceptions of the work of the district office personnel

and their lack of fiscal responsibility. The district and provincial surveys of parent satisfaction also indicated a gap between perceptions of individual schools and the district as a whole, with the district ranking below typical districts in the province.

Most importantly, Chen learned that human resource performance management policies, even ones that are generally well-written, can be difficult for large districts to implement in an ethical manner. And, in some circumstances, they can be weaponized to threaten employees regardless of the work role, leadership position, or positive evaluations and reputation of the employee.

Questions to Consider

- How does the ethic of justice apply to this situation?
- How does the ethic of care relate to this leadership vignette? How might it hinder or support the ethic of justice?
- Thinking about the Shapiro and Stefkovich multiparadigm framework (2022), how does the ethic of the profession apply to this vignette?
- Was it ethical for the director to tell Chen that the letter of reprimand would not be put in Chen's employment file, but instead be housed in his desk and the desk of the HR associate director?
- Which of the signs of a toxic work culture were evident in this vignette?
- Which of Sutton's remedies might leaders consider to improve this workplace culture?

Who you are is speaking so loudly that I can't hear what you're saying.
—Ralph Waldo Emerson, former American essayist, philosopher, and abolitionist

These vignettes and voices of educators articulate the depth of impact from unethical employee behavior and toxic educational workplaces. However, this is not to say that all schools and school districts are impacted in the same way—there are many ethical school leaders who are skillfully, and often fiercely, able to create and maintain positive school cultures. And, they see the impact of their work in a happy, collaborative, and productive staff, in students who know their teachers are able to focus on their learning, and in parents who trust their schools and school districts to do the "right [educational] things" for their children.

In our next and final chapter, we will provide vignettes of leadership practice and the voices of impacted educators from healthy educational workplace cultures. This final chapter will also provide next steps and future considerations to create and maintain ethical school and school district leadership practices which contribute to healthy workplace cultures.

References

Epitropoulos, A. (2019). 10 signs of a toxic school culture. *Educational Leadership, 61*(9) https://www.ascd.org/el/articles/10-signs-of-a-toxic-school-culture

Kusy, M. (2018a). *Why I don't work here anymore: A leader's guide to offset the financial and emotional costs of toxic employees.* CRC Press/Taylor & Francis Group.

Kusy, M. (2018b). Why I don't work here anymore: Leader beware. *Leader to Leader*, 1–6. https://www.mitchellkusy.com/wp-content/uploads/2018/06/Kusy-2018-Leader_to_Leader.pdf

Kusy, M., & Holloway, E. (2009). *Toxic workplace!: Managing toxic personalities and their systems of power.* Jossey-Bass.

Northouse, P. (2022). *Leadership: Theory and practice* (9th ed.). Sage Publications.

Shapiro, J., & Stefkovich, J. (2022). *Ethical leadership and decision making in education: Applying theoretical perspectives to complex dilemmas* (5th ed.). https://doi.org/10.4324/9781003022862

Sutton, R. (2010). *The no asshole rule: Building a civilized workplace and surviving one that isn't.* Grand Central Publishing.

Sutton, R. (2017). *The asshole survival guide: How to deal with people who treat you like dirt.* Houghton Mifflin Harcourt.

CHAPTER 7

Leadership Lessons from Healthy Educational Workplace Cultures

Abstract In this chapter, we provide examples of what have been described to us by educators as their experiences with ethical leadership in healthy school and school district cultures. Again, the examples in this chapter include educators who are from three different levels in the typical hierarchy of school districts—teachers, principals, and superintendents/directors. Each example includes a vignette of their experience, as well as their reflections on the impacts of the ethical leadership behavior and healthy workplace culture on their productivity and wellness, on their students, and on school district effectiveness and credibility in their larger communities. Each of the examples also includes questions for reader reflection. The intent of this final chapter is to leave readers with next steps and future considerations to create and maintain ethical school and school district leadership approaches which contribute to healthy workplace cultures.

Keywords Vignettes of leadership practice • Educator voices • Healthy school cultures • Responsibility-centered leadership • Impact of ethical educational leadership

> "You can do what I cannot do. I can do what you cannot do. Together we can do great things."
> —Mother Teresa, former Albanian-Indian Catholic nun

© The Author(s), under exclusive license to Springer Nature Switzerland AG 2024
B. Yee, D. Yee, *International Perspectives on Ethical Educational Leadership*, https://doi.org/10.1007/978-3-031-70839-8_7

In this chapter, we provide examples of what have been described to us by educators as their experiences with ethical leadership in healthy school and school district cultures. Again, the examples in this chapter include educators who are from three different levels in the typical hierarchy of school districts—teachers, principals, and superintendents/directors. Each example includes a vignette of their experience, as well as their reflections on the impacts of the ethical leadership behavior and healthy workplace culture on their productivity and wellness, on their students, and on school district effectiveness and credibility in their larger communities. Each of the examples also includes questions for reader reflection. The intent of this final chapter is to leave readers with lessons learned, next steps, and future considerations to create and maintain ethical school and school district leadership approaches which contribute to healthy workplace cultures.

Healthy Workplace Cultures

So, how does this ethical leadership and educational workplace culture discussion end in a positive way, based on the discussion of toxic workplace cultures in the previous chapter? In his work on creating positive and respectful teams and organizations, Stanford professor Bob Sutton (2010) indicated that "there is so much evidence that civilized workplaces are not a naïve dream, that they do exist, and that pervasive contempt can be erased and replaced with mutual respect when a team or organization is managed right" (p. 6).

Sutton (2010) explained that "organizations that drive in compassion and drive out fear, attract superior talent, have lower turnover costs, share ideas more freely, have less dysfunctional internal competition and trump the external competition" (p. 170). His view was that companies can actually gain a competitive advantage by "giving their people personal respect, training them to be effective and humane managers, allowing them time and resources to take care of themselves and their families,...and making it safe to express concerns" (p. 170). His perspective certainly resonates with our experiences as educators and leaders in school districts—and with the views and experiences of educational leaders who we have worked with in schools in Canada, the United States, Finland, and Germany.

Healthy School and School District Cultures

In the literature and in our experience (and, also as educators have described to us), an organizational culture will be healthy or toxic depending on the interactions between the people in the organization. In schools and school districts with healthy workplace cultures there are many overlapping and cohesive interactions among all members of the organization (Shafer, 2018).

Typically, healthy school cultures are characterized by:

- Ethical leadership: Effective, ethical leadership is key in fostering healthy school and school district cultures. Leaders should motivate and inspire both staff members and students; and, their values and actions need to align with those of the school and the district.
- Shared goals and values: A healthy school culture is characterized by shared goals and vision. Everyone in the school community should have a clear understanding of where the school and school district are heading and what they are committed to achieve.
- Inclusive and diverse community: Healthy school and school district cultures value and promote diversity, equity, and inclusion. Individual employee and student differences are valued as assets to enrich the learning organization. This can be observed in inclusive hiring practices, effective diversity policies, and a culture that values different perspectives.
- Positive and respectful relationships: Healthy school cultures demonstrate respectful relationships among students, teachers, principals, parents, and the wider community. This includes strong student-staff connections, where teachers endeavor to know students on a personal level. Students and staff feel physically and emotionally safe, able to express themselves without judgment or discipline.
- Honest, open, and transparent communication: The extent to which school provides an opportunity to share information and provide feedback is the key to creating a culture that fosters positive interaction between the community members. This honest and open communication promotes the development of a healthy school culture and trusting school community.
- Positive and responsive learning environment: A healthy school culture provides a learning environment which nurtures the intellectual, social, emotional, and physical development of students. This

includes flexibility, access to appropriate resources, and openness to innovative learning strategies/processes.
- Continuous improvement valued: A positive school culture is characterized by a commitment to continuous improvement. The school has high expectations (along with appropriate support) which encourage students and staff members to be confident life- and career-long learners. This includes regular assessments and adjustments to enhance the school's learning environment and culture.
- Active engagement: In a healthy school culture, staff members, students, and parents are very involved in building the community. This includes positive participation in school and school district activities and a commitment to improve the school's culture.
- Wellness treated as a key priority: A healthy school culture promotes mental health and overall well-being for both students and staff members, which involves creating quality student-teacher relationships to foster a sense of belonging. For staff members, this can include the district offering wellness programs and mental health resources as commitments to employees.

One Teacher's Experience

The first teaching experiences of a teacher often have a large impact on the rest of their career—that was Jenny's experience. *When I was doing my final two years of university study for my teaching degree, I had the opportunity to work in two different school districts for my practicum placements because of their proximity to my university. In one of the districts, my first placement was quite strained and stressful with a male physical education teacher who was very traditional and rigid in his approach to his students—and, to me as a practicum teacher. In fact, I felt this teacher was only interested in having a student teacher so he could spend more time on his computer in the physical education office or running personal errands, rather than observing me and assisting me to do a good job with his students.*

After that experience I was quite nervous about my next practicum placement. What I found was a welcoming and dynamic team who wanted to help me become a great teacher, even though I was placed in a large high school with a very competitive physical education department head who loved coaching his high school football team as much as he loved teaching his sports performance and activity classes. Jenny explained that this practicum experience provided her with an opportunity to work with the department head's classes and also classes of other members of the physical education team. She often had the opportunity to engage in collaborative planning with the team, which included teachers who had taught at the school for many years as well as teachers who were quite new to the profession. There was always something interesting happening at the school in terms of curriculum-based field trips, extracurricular activities, and athletic events. And, she had the opportunity to get to know the principal and assistant principals of the school who were interested in coming into her classes to observe her working with students. *We were a very competitive phys ed department—always joking and having fun, and also thinking up pranks to play on the other departments! When my practicum ended in April, I continued to volunteer at the school until the end of the year to help out that phys ed team and other colleagues who had welcomed me and taught me so much in a short time!*

When she finished her teaching degree, Jenny applied to teach in that district because of the positive experience that she had in her practicum. She was hired at one of their middle schools and began working with a principal and assistant principal who encouraged the positive energy and passion she brought to her work every day, with both students and other staff members. She felt comfortable asking them questions and bringing them her dilemmas regarding students, parents, and other colleagues. At the end of her first year, they nominated her for the district award for beginning teachers. Because they really knew her as a professional and as a person, they were able to eloquently describe her journey as a first-year teacher—and, she won the award.

Although Jenny has moved on to other schools and into leadership roles as her career has progressed, she explained that she often thinks back to her experiences with the engaged and ethical leaders in this district as her "North Star" to guide her work with her staff members.

The Teacher's Reflections

On Staff Member Wellness, as Well as Employee Development and Productivity
In her first year as a teacher, Jenny found herself immersed in an environment that defied the stereotypical challenges associated with educational organizations. From the very beginning, the administrative team at Elmwood Middle School displayed an unwavering commitment to the

well-being and growth of their staff. The principal, Mr. Bell, fostered an atmosphere of open communication and genuine care. Monthly check-ins with new teachers were not just about evaluation and accountability but served as an opportunity for teachers to voice concerns and share ideas. It was more than classroom observations that needed to happen for contractual purposes; it was a genuine demonstration of leadership and mentorship, ensuring that Jenny had the tools she needed for a long and successful career. The support extended beyond the classroom, with regular staff wellness events and workshops focusing on what the staff identified as their needs. Jenny felt valued and empowered, realizing that her success was intertwined with the school's dedication to the holistic development of its educators.

This early experience at Elmwood Middle School set the foundation for Jenny's flourishing career in education. The supportive administrative team not only prioritized the academic success of the students but also recognized the crucial role that teacher well-being played in achieving those goals. As the years unfolded, Jenny continued to thrive, embracing opportunities for professional development and collaboration. The positive culture at Elmwood Middle School shaped her teaching philosophy, instilling in her a deep appreciation for the interconnectedness of personal and professional growth. Inspired by the mentorship she received during those formative years, Jenny knew she wanted to become a principal providing that same level of support for her teachers and students—creating a ripple effect that echoed the values she had first experienced in that remarkably nurturing school environment.

On Student Learning Outcomes

As a new teacher at Elmwood Middle School, Jenny was struck by the palpable sense of support and inclusivity that permeated the halls of the school. Principal Bell prioritized creating an environment where every student felt seen and valued. Jenny was particularly inspired by the school's dedication to supporting the diverse group of students, including a significant number from the nearby First Nations reserve. The school provided specialized training to help teachers understand and respect the cultural nuances of those students, fostering an environment where everyone felt valued and understood. This support allowed Jenny to focus not only on delivering a robust curriculum but also on tailoring her teaching methods to meet the unique needs of her diverse student body. Jenny later went on to be the First Nations education coordinator, acting as a liaison between the First Nations Elders and the school to ensure the voice of the First Nations community was honored in their children's education.

The collaborative spirit at Elmwood Middle School extended beyond the classroom. Regular team meetings facilitated open discussions about effective strategies for engaging students and their families from the nearby First Nations reserve, ensuring that teachers had the resources and knowledge to provide a meaningful and culturally responsive education for all students. Team meetings were often held on the reserve to facilitate family involvement in the children's education. Jenny witnessed firsthand the positive impact of this approach as her students flourished academically and emotionally. The supportive environment allowed her to not only connect with her students on a deeper level but also their families—and contribute to the broader goal of creating an inclusive and enriching educational experience for all. This early experience set the tone for the rest of Jenny's teaching career, instilling in her a commitment to embracing diversity and ensuring that every student felt seen, heard, capable, and empowered in the learning process.

On Parent and Community Perceptions of School District Effectiveness
In Jenny's view, the positive and supportive environment cultivated at Elmwood Middle School had a profound impact on how parents and the broader community perceived the effectiveness of the school and the district. The school's commitment to transparency and involving parents in the educational journey of their children fostered a strong sense of trust. Parent-teacher conferences, workshops designed to help families understand what was impacting their child's education, and school-community events showcased the collaborative spirit of Elmwood Middle School. As a result, parents felt actively engaged in their children's education; and, the community at large viewed the school as a pillar of success. Jenny believed that this positive perception was not only a testament to the school's commitment to academic excellence but also a reflection of its dedication to building strong relationships with parents and the community.

Most importantly from her practicum placement and her first-year teaching, Jenny learned early in her career that the quality of relationships with colleagues and leaders can have either a negative or positive impact on teacher confidence and well-being. She learned that when teachers feel physically and emotionally safe and are able to ask questions and express themselves without judgment, they are able to approach the difficult job of teaching with a mindset of professional growth and development. She also learned the importance of open, honest, and culturally respectful communication with parents in support of student learning and relationship building. She experienced firsthand examples of ethical leaders who inspired and motivated both staff members and students; those leaders became role models that she sought to emulate as she moved into leadership roles in her own career.

Questions to Consider

- How does the ethic of care apply in this teacher's experience?
- Thinking about the Shapiro and Stefkovich multiparadigm framework (2022), how does the ethic of the profession apply in this situation?
- Which of the characteristics of a healthy workplace culture were evident in this vignette?

ONE PRINCIPAL'S EXPERIENCE

When Bianca's husband accepted a promotion that involved moving their family to another state, she was happy for him and for their family as a whole. But she was unsure of how she would navigate moving to another leadership position in a new school district in the middle of her career as an educator. She had worked in the previous district as a classroom teacher, a resource teacher, a vice-principal, and had also been a school principal for a several years. *I just knew how everything worked in that district…who to connect with and who to avoid. I understood the quirks of the senior leaders and had been allowed the autonomy to support and develop my school staff to create a really positive school culture focused on responsive pedagogy in order to meet the needs of our very diverse student population. I knew I had to do my employment search well in order to find a district where I could develop further my leadership practice because I was just beginning a doctoral program in educational leadership. I knew that my university courses and research would be more impactful and authentic if there was alignment between my leadership approaches and the senior leaders and school board in the district I worked for. Because we were moving to a large urban area, I also knew that there were a number of possible school districts for me to apply to.*

Bianca started by reviewing the websites of each of the districts to see what the priorities of the districts were and what their vision, mission, and strategic plans said about their current and future work. She knew from her previous university studies and her work as a leader that there are always multiple layers to the culture of school districts—what is the public face of the district and its espoused values? And, how would their teachers and parents describe the real work of the district? And finally, what were the deeply embedded and unspoken beliefs about teaching, learning, and leadership in the district? After a careful look at each of the four districts, she was surprised how different the districts were in portraying themselves publicly regarding student learning, employee career development, and leadership ethics and priorities. She was drawn to two of the districts because of their potential connection to her expertise and professional interests. She applied to those districts after having a conversation with the directors of their HR departments about what type of leaders they were hoping to hire in their principal cohort—and how they developed their principals into senior system leaders.

Bianca was offered interviews for a principal position in both of those districts. Both interviews were conducted in a thoughtful way by their interview panels. Bianca felt that she was able to ask key questions of those panels and receive honest answers. The senior leaders of both districts explained that their student populations were becoming more diverse and that the COVID-19 pandemic had created learning gaps for their most vulnerable students. They were both able to describe making some good progress to improve learning for all students but that their districts were "not quite there yet." They indicated that they needed school-based leaders who were passionate about improving learning for students and professional learning for teachers—and they acknowledged the work of a school principal was complex and difficult.

I was very encouraged by my interviews with both school districts and knew that I could find a place to have a positive impact on student learning and teacher pedagogy in either one. Both districts offered her a principal position. Ultimately her decision was made because of an interaction that she had during the interview process with one of the district superintendents. The superintendent explained that their district's focus on well-being for students and staff members coming out of the COVID-19 pandemic was lived out in the daily decision-making of board members and senior leaders—in the allocation of additional resources to support programming for both students and employees, through careful policy development and implementation, and by working closely with union partners to manage the workload of teachers, principals, and support staff. Bianca felt senior leaders knew they had to "put their money where their mouth was" to appropriately care for their students, families, and employees.

Two years into this new principal role, Bianca knows that she has developed further as an ethical leader because of the support and modeling from senior leaders in this district.

The Principal's Reflections

On Staff Member Wellness, as Well as Employee Development and Productivity

One of the reasons that Bianca decided to work in this district was the leadership development programs that the district offered its principals. As a new leader to the district, the professional leadership learning sessions for principals were very important for her to continue to improve her leadership practice alongside her peers and to also develop a social network of critical friends. *One of the best things about the monthly principal leadership learning sessions is our K-12 format where principals across the district develop our understanding of the continuum of student learning supports and teacher practices in the district—how we actually have more similarities than differences across the levels. In my last district, elementary principals almost always only met with other elementary principals; and, the conversation quite often was about how we cared for and supported our students and families so well and then that was all lost when students went on to middle and high school (with none of our senior school colleagues present to inform our discussion.)* In addition to these leadership learning sessions, Bianca explained that principals who aspired to move to more senior leadership roles in the district were assisted by HR advisors to develop a district portfolio and then be able to participate in a cohort led by senior leaders. These leadership learning sessions followed an action research approach where principals brought evidence of student learning and teacher practice in their schools to problem solve with their principal peers and senior leaders, focusing on continuous improvement.

On Student Learning Outcomes

In this new school, Bianca explained that she has a much more diverse student population than she did in her previous school. Because of her ongoing doctoral studies, she has been learning about culturally responsive pedagogy and culturally responsive leadership practices. In fact, she is focusing her dissertation research on improved student engagement and achievement as a result of students feeling they are confident learners in schools that honor and celebrate the diversity of their learning community. *When I arrived here, I knew that I had to learn more about how to assist our teachers to work with our families who have recently come to our country. When I talked with teachers, they described how food and housing insecurity seemed to be impacting student attendance and student ability to be fully present in their classrooms. Teachers were also concerned that they did not have time to get to know their families well enough to develop a trusting relationship—and to also support students and families whose first language was not English. I knew I had to work with them to stop some of the traditional teaching practices that were not serving their students well and to replace them with more culturally responsive strategies. And, I needed to lead this school in a more culturally responsive way than I had in previous schools. We've had some very honest conversations about what we need to stop doing and how to see students and their families with "different eyes." We're already seeing increased student and family connection to our school, and I'm confident improvement in student learning outcomes will follow.*

On Parent and Community Perceptions of School District Effectiveness
The district where Bianca works is one of the smaller districts in the large urban area. It has been well known to the community for providing a high-quality education to students for many years, with graduates being accepted into a mixture of colleges and universities in the area. During the COVID-19 pandemic and after thoughtful consultation with parents, the district moved to a hybrid learning format where they paid particular attention to their most vulnerable students and families, providing both in-person and online resources and supports. Bianca explained that when all students were able to return to in-person learning, parents stayed with the district where in other districts a number of families chose to have their children continue to learn online. *During that really difficult pandemic time for students, parents, and staff, our school district efforts to support families was noticed by the community members and businesses who provided whatever additional resources they could to help our students —from food, to school supplies, books, and technologies, to having employees who were working from home volunteer to connect online with students.*

Most importantly, Bianca learned the true importance of thoughtful reflection and ethical leader action related to diversity, equity, and inclusion. In her previous leadership experiences, she had thought she was doing a good job in this area. Coming into this new principal role impacted by COVID-19 and learning from her doctoral program reading and coursework, she knew she needed to do more so that employee and student diversity were strong assets to enrich her new learning community. Supported by the inclusive hiring practices and effective DEI policies that were well understood across her district, she was able to connect in more meaningful ways with her parent community—all to improve student learning. She also experienced working with a senior leadership team who were able to work effectively with their board to develop shared goals for district improvement, as well as clearly communicate their commitment to achieving those goals throughout the organization. As a result, she was able to observe honest and open communication strategies and processes to further develop her own healthy school culture and trusting school community.

Questions to Consider

- How do the ethics of care and critique apply in this leader's experience?
- Thinking about the Shapiro and Stefkovich multiparadigm framework (2022), how does the ethic of the profession apply in this situation?
- Which of the characteristics of a healthy workplace culture were evident in this vignette?

ONE SUPERINTENDENT'S EXPERIENCE

After years of working in several different school districts, when I moved into this district, I knew it was just meant to be. I had wanted to work there for a number of years because I had heard good things about the district; and, my elderly father, who also lived in that location, needed more of my individual support. (The district I was working for was too far away to get to him quickly if he had a medical issue.) Then I saw an advertisement for a superintendent position related to inclusive education posted in the newspaper and I thought, "Are they kidding? They never post externally. They always hire from within." I had contacted their HR department several years before when I contemplated moving to the area, but their director had told me that I needed to be a district employee to apply for a leadership position. I always have a resume ready so when I saw this posting, I put together a quick cover letter and added a few photos of me working with principals and teachers. I sent the information off electronically--and thought I would never hear another thing about it, based on my previous experiences.

When Clark received a call from the district HR director the next week to set up an interview, they were very surprised. They were sent the questions that the superintendents would be asking during the interview and also asked if there were samples of their work in other districts that they would like to bring to share with the interview team. Again, Clark mentioned that it was a very different reception and conversation than what they had with the previous HR director. When they went to the interview, they felt welcome. It was obvious that the interview panel had read their documents and had talked with their references because they complimented them on their long history of excellent work in other districts. The panel indicated that they were very happy that Clark was considering their district as a place to lead.

Clark explained that the interview didn't feel like the "typical Spanish Inquisition" interview but instead became a deep professional dialogue about leadership—and teaching and student learning. Because of discussion and follow up questions, it was clear that the interviewers were very well read related to current educational leadership literature and were able to truly understand the complexities of the work in the superintendent position that Clark was applying for. They left the interview feeling that this would be a position which would stretch their abilities, allowing them to lead and to learn with appropriate peer and supervisor support. When they were offered the position, they gratefully accepted.

Clark described the district onboarding process as very thoughtful, albeit time-consuming. They had the opportunity to meet with each person on the senior leadership team individually, to ask questions about their portfolios, and to begin to understand them as school district leaders—and the culture of the district itself.

A year into their tenure, Clark explained that they are further energized by the direction that the board of trustees and executive team are moving the district. There is no question that the work hours are long, and the problems are very complex—but they reflected that it never feels like they have to "do it all themselves." They explained that they have been able to build their inclusive education group into a powerful team willing to honestly reflect on their work and to make changes that would improve the educational environment for classroom teachers, so that they could do their best work with students.

I knew from the interview it was just the right match for me—and my family. Really a place that I could continue to grow and develop my passion for leading system teams so that each student in the district would ultimately have the learning experience that their parents would describe as respectful, engaging, and excellent.

The Superintendent's Reflections

On Staff Member Wellness, as Well as Employee Development and Productivity

Clark explained that as they began to understand the culture of the district, it was clear that when the trustees had approved a new district vision and mission statement which articulated the importance of staff member well-being and career development, they were also willing to allocate the financial and human resources to create effective systems and processes to support those aspirations. The human resources advisor team was very skilled in supporting superintendents and principals working with staff members who had physical or mental health issues. Clark also noticed the respectful working relationships with the teacher and support staff union in this district, even though there was the typical labor relations posturing during collective bargaining periods.

On Student Learning Outcomes

In the province where Clark works, the ministry does not have a provincial standardized testing program. While there has been some discussion about creating one similar to other Canadian provinces, there is a history of parent trust in the work of teachers in their local schools. Assessment of curriculum implementation by the ministry has involved sampling student work for the purpose of improving instruction, reflecting their spirit of continuous improvement. The district where Clark works focuses on classroom assessment practices which provide multiple and varied opportunities for students to demonstrate their learning, with particular attention to the success of Indigenous students. Teachers assess provincial curriculum outcomes using a balanced approach and triangulation of multiple types of evidence of student learning. *I feel very fortunate to not have to deal with parent concerns related to the ranking of our schools and schools 'marketing themselves for survival' based on standardized test scores.*

On Parent and Community Perceptions of School District Effectiveness
As superintendent of the department which oversees inclusive education, Clark described how they were the district leader who reviewed and adjudicated all parent complaints related to programming for students with exceptional learning needs. If parents were unhappy with their response, parents had a recourse to contact the minister of education. Clark had also worked in another district in a similar position and by comparison, the number of complaints that came to their office in this district was very minor. *Here the school principals, with the support of my inclusive education team, are almost always able to work to a positive solution with parents who have concerns regarding the specialized programming and supports for their children—so I don't have to become involved.* In fact, the staff members at the ministry had recently contacted Clark to thank them and their team for their positive approaches to the very diverse group of parents in the district. In addition, Clark indicated that parents' positive perceptions of individual school and school district effectiveness was one of the highest in the province, as measured by their provincial parent survey.

In terms of "lessons learned" most importantly, Clark realized the impact that individual senior leaders have on individual employee satisfaction and overall district credibility. As a senior leader seeking employment with the district, they had very different experiences with different leaders and those experiences reinforced Clark's perspective that every individual deserves ethical, compassionate treatment in our educational systems. Also in the district onboarding process, it was reinforced that positive relationship and culture building takes intention, skill, and time—something that Clark was able to translate into building their inclusive education team. Clark also developed further understanding about senior leaders demonstrating a transparent "continuous improvement mindset" with high expectations and appropriate support which encourages students and staff members to be confident life- and career-long learners and builds positive relationships with parents and communities.

Questions to Consider

- How does the ethic of care apply in this leader's experience?
- Thinking about the Shapiro and Stefkovich multiparadigm framework (2022), how does the ethic of the profession apply in this situation?

- Which of the characteristics of a healthy workplace culture were evident in this vignette?

Next Steps and Future Considerations

We hope that you leave this book with the perspective that ethical educational leadership matters to leaders themselves, to their schools and districts, and to their communities—and that you are more curious about leadership ethics and how they impact your work in education.

Also, we would leave you with these key considerations:

- As educational leaders, we are in the "people business," and fostering ethical relationships is important to individual and group well-being, to positive school culture, and to district success.
- Creating a healthy school district culture requires ethical leadership from many individuals and groups within the organization. We have explored the ethical leadership of trustees and school boards, district leaders such as superintendents and directors, and school principals as key agents in formal leadership roles. We believe that acknowledging and developing teacher leaders is an important component of the ethic of the profession for educators who hold informal leadership roles; certainly, it is in the best interests of students (Shapiro & Stefkovich, 2022).
- Ethical educational leadership requires moral courage, as Shields (2020) and others have indicated. (We have a poster that has been in our office for many years which says "Courage is what it takes to stand up and speak. Courage is also what it takes to sit down and listen." We believe ethical educational leadership requires both types of moral courage.)
- The concept of "emotional contagion" as described in organizational psychology research applies to school and school district workplace cultures and needs to be understood and carefully managed by educational leaders.
- Educational leaders are always being observed for consistency between their words and their behaviors, and modeling ethical behavior becomes even more critical as leaders move up in their school district hierarchy. (And also, as leaders become more senior in their districts, they often become less reflective or aware of their leadership behaviors and the impacts on their individual employees and employee groups.)

- Educational leaders seeking ethical actions and developing policy in an ethical manner must carefully understand and honor their local community, provincial/state, and national contexts. (For example, in our work in Canada, we have observed and experienced numerous examples of leaders' "policy/practice borrowing" from an American source which have not fit in their Canadian educational context. And, those initiatives have failed in implementation, having a negative impact on workplace culture.)

In his book, *The Motive*, Patrick Lencioni (2020) eloquently describes ethical leadership in a way that resonates with us. The premise of the book is that there are two fundamental motives for people to become leaders. He explains that reward-centered leadership is demonstrated by leaders who are motivated by personal rewards. Leadership becomes individual work for rewards such as status, power, money, or the "biggest office in the building." They see leadership as a prize for years of hard work and are drawn by the possibilities for attention and status. Lencioni explains that this motive can lead to the avoidance of unpleasant situations and gritty, but important, daily activities required of ethical leadership, leaving the people they lead without appropriate support, guidance, and direction. In contrast, Lencioni explains that responsibility-centered leadership is demonstrated by leaders who believe that their role is one of service to others and to their community. This type of leader is willing to engage in difficult, uncomfortable, and sometimes mundane activities for the good of the people they lead and to elevate the moral purpose and ethics of their organization. They see leadership as a duty to serve and collaboratively support their staff in becoming team members and leaders. Lencioni offers valuable insights to help leaders find their true purpose and avoid the pitfalls that can impact the people they lead and their organizations in negative ways.

As Lencioni ends the book, he leaves readers with this call to action:

> It's long past the time that we, as individuals and as a society, reestablish the standard that leadership can never be about the leader more than the led…If we can restore the collective attitude that leadership is meant to be a joyfully difficult and selfless responsibility, I am convinced that we will see companies become more successful, employees more engaged and fulfilled, and society more optimistic and hopeful. (p. 170)

Certainly, Lencioni (2020) is writing for a corporate or business-oriented audience. In our experience, we have encountered both types of motivations in the school-based and district leaders we have worked with; and, we have always led from a responsibility-centered perspective—compassion, hard work, courage, and dedication to improving our learning communities.

What kind of leader will you be?

> *Not the cry, but the flight of a wild duck, leads the flock to fly and follow.*
> —Chinese proverb

References

Lencioni, P. (2020). *The motive: Why so many leaders abdicate their most important responsibilities.* Jossey-Bass.

Shafer, L. (2018). *What makes a good culture?* https://www.gse.harvard.edu/ideas/usable-knowledge/18/07/what-makes-good-school-culture

Shapiro, J., & Stefkovich, J. (2022). *Ethical leadership and decision making in education: Applying theoretical perspectives to complex dilemmas* (5th ed.). https://doi.org/10.4324/9781003022862

Shields, C. M. (2020). *Becoming a transformative leader: A guide to creating equitable schools (1st ed.).* Routledge. https://doi.org/10.4324/9780429261091

Sutton, R. (2010). *The no asshole rule: Building a civilized workplace and surviving one that isn't.* New Grand Central Publishing.

INDEX

C
Canada, 1–4, 11, 12, 14, 20, 23, 30, 31, 33, 37, 38, 44–46, 54–61, 65, 66, 70, 71, 73, 74, 83–90, 96, 97, 101, 115–122, 124, 126, 131, 147, 164, 179
Codes of conduct, 68, 93, 96, 124, 127, 137
Community perception, 3, 20, 31, 36, 142, 150–151, 156, 159–160, 169–170, 173–174, 177
Cultural norms, 21, 22, 129

D
Director, 11, 31, 37, 38, 46, 48, 83–111, 117, 132, 133, 142, 149, 156–161, 164, 171, 174, 175, 178

E
Education ministry, 44, 54–56, 61–67, 90, 103

Emotional contagion, 143, 178
Employee engagement, 20, 25, 26, 37–39
Ethical dilemmas, 2, 9, 10, 44, 77–78, 108–111
Ethical educational leadership, 6, 9–12, 20, 116, 129, 178
Ethical leadership, 1–14, 21, 31, 44, 45, 50–53, 57–59, 61, 67–68, 73–77, 83–108, 115–137, 164, 165, 178, 179

F
Finland, 1, 3, 4, 11, 12, 14, 20, 44, 45, 61–69, 83, 84, 96–101, 116, 127–131, 135, 136, 164

G
Germany, 1, 3, 4, 11, 12, 14, 20, 44, 45, 69–77, 83, 84, 100–108, 116, 124–127, 131, 134, 164

H

Healthy school culture, 29, 33–35, 165, 166, 174
Healthy workplace culture, 5, 22, 23, 25–26, 28, 39, 58, 78, 83, 161, 164, 165, 170, 174, 178

I

Instructional leadership, 2, 12–14, 116, 119, 123, 129, 148, 156

L

Leader credentials, 87
Leadership framework, 4, 5, 118, 129, 131
Leadership paradigm, 9–12
Leadership standards, 13, 50–52, 57–59, 67–68, 73–75, 84–108, 116–131, 134, 137, 156

M

Moral leadership, 88, 89, 120

O

Organizational culture, 20–23, 28, 31, 165
Organizational psychology, 4, 19, 20, 23, 30, 142, 143, 145, 178

P

Parent perception, 156
Professional organizations, 86, 89, 92

S

School board, 4, 11, 44–78, 83–86, 91–93, 98, 100, 108, 122, 154, 178
School district effectiveness, 36, 142, 150–151, 156, 159–160, 164, 169–170, 173–174, 177

School effectiveness, 36, 125
School principal, 5, 11, 12, 37, 85, 98–101, 105, 108, 115–137, 147, 150, 151, 157, 170, 171, 177, 178
Social information processing (SIP), 8
Student achievement, 34, 49, 59, 60, 157
Student learning outcomes, 19–20, 31, 142, 150, 155–156, 159, 168–169, 172–173, 176
Superintendent, 11, 31, 37, 46, 83–111, 120, 151, 171, 176

T

Teacher
  employee productivity, 19, 31–33, 142, 150, 167–168, 172
  employee professional development, 31–33
  employee wellness, 31–33
Toxic school culture, 9, 19, 20, 142, 144, 145
Toxic workplace culture, 19, 23–36, 39, 78, 116, 142–144, 155, 164
Trustee
  board member, 4, 44, 51–53, 59, 61, 65, 67–68, 75, 77–78
  commissioner, 59, 61

U

Unethical leadership, 7, 142, 143, 155
United States (US), 1–4, 11, 12, 14, 20, 23, 30–33, 44–55, 57, 58, 60, 65, 71, 73, 74, 83, 84, 91–97, 101, 107, 115, 116, 122–124, 126, 131, 164

V

Vignettes of leadership practice, 3, 14, 161

SPRINGER NATURE

GPSR Compliance

The European Union's (EU) General Product Safety Regulation (GPSR) is a set of rules that requires consumer products to be safe and our obligations to ensure this.

If you have any concerns about our products, you can contact us on ProductSafety@springernature.com

In case Publisher is established outside the EU, the EU authorized representative is:

Springer Nature Customer Service Center GmbH
Europaplatz 3
69115 Heidelberg, Germany

The manufacturer's authorised representative in the EU is Springer Nature Customer Service Centre GmbH, Europaplatz 3, 69115 Heidelberg, Germany. If you have any concerns regarding our products, please contact ProductSafety@springernature.com

Printed and bound by CPI Group (UK) Ltd, Croydon, CR0 4YY
03/02/2025
01830398-0001